A TASTE OF
BURGUNDY

A TASTE OF
BURGUNDY

JULIAN & CAREY MORE

ABBEVILLE PRESS

NEW YORK LONDON PARIS

In memory of Alexandre Dumaine

First published in United States of America in 1993 by
ABBEVILLE PRESS
488 Madison Avenue, New York, NY 10022.

First published in Great Britain in 1993 by
PAVILION BOOKS LIMITED
196 Shaftesbury Avenue, London WC2H 8JL

Printed and bound in Hong Kong by Mandarin Offset

ISBN 1-55859-464-7

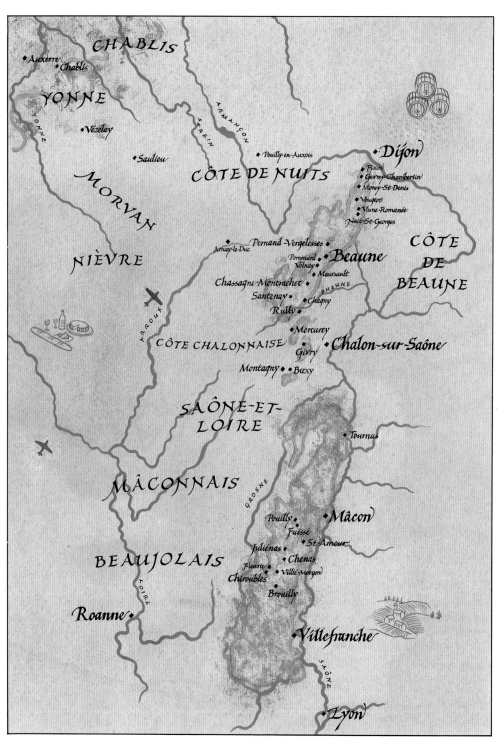

CHABLIS

• Auxerre • Chablis

YONNE

• Vézelay

• Saulieu

• Pouilly-en-Auxois

CÔTE DE NUITS

• Dijon

Fixin
• Gevrey-Chambertin
• Morey-St-Denis

• Vougeot
• Vosne-Romanée
• Nuit-St-Georges

MORVAN

NIÈVRE

Pernand-Vergelesses
• Arnay-le-Duc
Pommard • • Beaune
Volnay
• Meursault
Chassagne-Montrachet
Santenay • • Chagny
Rully

CÔTE DE NUITS

CÔTE DE BEAUNE

Mercurey •
CÔTE CHALONNAISE
Givry •

• Chalon-sur-Saône

Montagny • • Buxy

SAÔNE-ET-LOIRE

• Tournus

MÂCONNAIS

Pouilly • • Mâcon
Fuissé
• St-Amour
Juliénas •
• Chenas
BEAUJOLAIS
Fleurie
Chiroubles • • Villié-Morgon

• Brouilly

Roanne •

• Villefranche

• Lyon

Burgundy

 principal wine growing areas

Contents

COUNTRY FARE

Lucky Burgundy – producing such milk, she can
be called the mother of mankind.

ERASMUS

Our Burgundy began with breakfast. Normally one of France's duller repasts, but where better to redeem itself than the Hotel Côte d'Or, Saulieu?

Chez Bernard Loiseau, one of Burgundy's Big Six chefs, breakfast is a gentle introduction to his maverick talents. His is the new taste of Burgundy, yet with elegant simplicity came strictly country fare, served in a flowery garden. On *soignée* trays, the good old tastes all too rare even in France – farm butter, *jambon de Morvan* (the exquisite local ham), *velouté de brebis* (ewe's milk yogurt), eggs warm from the hen, home-baked bread and jams of chestnut, raspberries and blackberries from forest, garden and hedgerow.

Saulieu seemed the perfect place to start – in the heartland of Burgundy's gastronomy. Focal point of this vast province, it has a tradition very much its own, despite a mere 3183 inhabitants.

A foodie's paradise since the seventeenth century when it was a posting station on the Paris–Lyons road, now Saulieu is a pleasant detour from the *Autoroute du Soleil*. Rabelais celebrated its good cheer; Madame de Sévigné overdosed on its addictive *oeufs en meurette* (eggs in a red wine sauce), and was carried to her hotel room in a swoon.

After a sober breakfast at the Côte d'Or, we headed past François Pompon's glossy bronze statue of a Charolais bull to the *Journées Gourmandes du Grand Morvan*, a gastronomic fair held every May. Bernard Loiseau was honorary president, and our friend the mayor, Doctor Philippe Lavault, led officials from Dijon and Beaune round the stands of farmers, wine-makers and shopkeepers.

Here was a microcosm of Burgundian treats in store. Baker Poisot had fashioned the coat-of-arms of Saulieu in bread. Pisciculturists were handing out samples of smoked trout and carp from ponds at their nearby *château*. Jam-maker Jacques

Selim was like a wizard, manically stirring his steaming pan. There was honey from the Morvan hills, goat's cheeses gaily coloured with tarragon, paprika, cumin and cinders. Monsieur Perreau's ham ('Pork is good for the brain!') rivalled Monsieur Lapré's foie gras ('A little cholesterol never did anyone any harm!'). But none could rival Dame Alice, queening it in an Ascot hat, with her secret recipe for *pain d'epice*, whispering just a hint of it with lavender-honeyed breath: 'No sugar, no preservatives, a grain of anis crushed, cinnamon.'

We were honouring defenders of French quality. From the server of snails at his counter to the restaurateurs of every category, all were enemies of hormone-fattened cattle and chemicalized wine and *le fast-food*.

Marc Millot, chef and owner of the Lion d'Or, had joined forces with Bernard Loiseau to create the night's menu for the fair's visitors. Loiseau and Millot, both young, are otherwise poles apart: Loiseau – media-conscious purveyor of luxury, rebel inventor in the kitchen, known by gourmets from Tokyo to San Francisco; Millot – hotel rooms basic, his name intentionally in no guide, his cuisine simpler and more traditional – beef and ham and chicken in sumptuous sauces. 'Morvan chicken, of course!' Marc told me, adding mockingly: 'The Bresse! Where's that?' Answer: where the best Burgundian poultry is supposed to come from. Regional rivalry is rife.

Bernard and Marc, whatever their differences, would defend local products to the last feather or trotter. That night, in total solidarity, they served a Morvan *pot au feu* (simmered meat stew with vegetables) of beef, chicken and foie gras. They are not blindly chauvinistic. 'Some local recipes are just too rustic,' Marc said. 'There's a crêpe called *crâpiau morvandelle* which is only good for balancing wardrobes.'

Balancing meals was easier. With the festive *pot au feu*, Marc would drink one of the lighter red Côte de Beaunes – Volnay, Monthélie, or Auxey-Duresses.

It was all a question of balance. If the cooks know their onions, forget the proverbial *crise de foie*. I had always imagined the Dukes of Burgundy slumped beneath the groaning board, and monks in Cistercian monasteries breaking their vows of silence with burps. Heavy, wintry, cooking with wine, cream, eggs and pork fat is designed to keep one warm in a Morvan blizzard here. I even saw snow on the hills near Pouilly-en-Auxois in May.

Well, the weather has not changed much, but eating habits certainly have. Vegetable oils (sunflower, walnut, colza, olive) and butter have replaced the pork fat. The French are among the least over-weight people in Europe. They drink less but better. And burgundy at its best (which is by no means always) is the finest wine in the world. Not everyone can afford the best, and some traditional recipes look quaintly extravagant today. On *very, very* special occasions in million-aire homes, however, Chambertin is still used to cook a cockerel. O Lucky Man and Bird!

There is another Burgundian cuisine, though – inventive, contemporary and beautifully presented. And typical of the New Burgundian style was the food at the Côte d'Or, where we were invited by the gourmet Mayor Lavault to experience Bernard Loiseau's *cuisine légère*.

Cuisine légère is a question of steaming vegetables and fruit to bring out their nat-ural flavours, rather than cooking them with salt or sugar. And Bernard keeps oil

and butter to a minimum, preferring nat-ural meat and fish juices instead. Much use of *suc* – what remains in the pan after sautéing – gives a superb lightness to rich-er dishes. But the portions are not mingy; Bernard has no patience with designer food. Good cooking to him is to feed healthy appetites healthily.

Our starters were pumpkin and basil soup, duck liver with fried crab apples; courgette (zucchini) flower with auber-gine (eggplant) 'caviare' in a juice of

Dame Alice – queen of pain d'épice *at the Saulieu Fair*

sweet peppers and artichoke mousse with a turtle-flavoured sauce and crisp potato flakes on top.

Carey gave me a taste of her John Dory with braised lettuce in veal sauce, the fish cooked on one side only. But I didn't know the Mayor well enough to whip a slice of his wild duck. And Madame Lavault was having the same as me: perch with *girolle* mushrooms.

Then, quite simply the best dessert I have ever tasted: *mille feuilles* with coffee

Traiteur Perreau's display at the Saulieu Fair

and chocolate, hot and cold between the crumbling pastry, with a chicory sauce. So light a butterfly could blow it away.

It was a fitting climax to the gastronomic fair at Saulieu. We visited others: more rural at Rouvray, more sophisticated at Dijon. In Burgundy, it's any excuse for a binge. Most famous are the *Trois Glorieuses*, a three-day annual marathon the third week in November. On Saturday, a six-course banquet at Clos de Vougeot where VIPs are elected to the wine brotherhood as Chevaliers du Tastevin; on Sunday, the charity wine auction in aid of the hospital at L'Hôtel Dieu, Beaune; on Monday, La Paulée at Meursault, a lunch where wine people

The arms of Saulieu sculpted in bread

bring rare vintages from their own cellars and offer them to each other in a spirit of lethal competitiveness. Tuesday, you hit the Perrier and rice cakes – or, more likely, a hair-of-the-dog and a nice plain *côte de boeuf*.

Mayor Lavault complained at the price even his friends at Meursult charge him per bottle. ('Three-hundred francs a friendly price? *Heinh!*') Many of these hot-ticket festivals in heavily restored, mock-medieval cellars are frankly commercial, an overhearty PR show put on for foreign guests. After the jollity and feasting, you may see a chevalier, his floppy hat askew, fumbling to get the keys of his BMW into the lock. Or a foreign wine-trade executive weaving down the street in search of his hotel.

During Saulieu's entirely unpretentious fair, Carey and I were well indoctrinated into the tastes ancient and modern of Burgundy and prepared to set forth on our journey.

*L'Hôtel Dieu,
Beaune –
medieval
building,
modern hospital*

SAUCES FOR COURSES

If you're not capable of a bit of magic, there's no point troubling yourself with cooking.
COLETTE

Before embarking on serious eating in Burgundy, a lack of knowledge about its sauces is like making the journey in a car with a wheel missing. Cooked mainly from what is produced locally – dairy products, mustard, wine – these accompaniments to meat, fish, game and vegetables give Burgundian cooking its special richness.

Classically, *à la bourguignonne* means made with burgundy. More precisely, *à la chablisienne* means made with Chablis, and in an ideal world the wine cooked in is the wine you serve with the dish. At today's burgundy prices (even with the recession slump at the 1991 Beaune auction), however, this can be unrealistic. Be of good cheer; an alternative is to cook with the nearest possible burgundy you can afford. Or, use foreign Pinot reds and Chardonnay whites of quality. Less expensive French reds should be full-bodied like Côtes du Rhône, Cahors, or Madirau. There are plenty of alternative cooking wines to burgundy. Consult your wine merchant.

In the most gastronomic of the four Burgundy departments, the Côte d'Or, the wrong side of the tracks means east of the N74 Dijon–Beaune road. The right side, where the great vineyard slopes meet the plain, is a name-drop of mighty reds: Fixin, Gevrey-Chambertin, Morey-St-Denis, Chambolle-Musigny, Vougeot, Flagey-Echézeaux, Vosne-Romanée, Nuits-St-Georges.

The wrong side is the poor benighted plain. But, for me, the wrong side is the right side for it contains a miraculous restaurant where Carey and I had our first experience of the Great Burgundian Sauce.

'*Café-Tabac*' was all the sign said. This off-putting frontage in the village of Flagey-Echézeaux disguised a dingy bar where a couple of *vignerons* were drowning their late-frost sorrows. The proprietor, Robert Losset, formerly a cross-Atlantic chef on the *France*, greeted us somewhat suspiciously. Foreigners? A woman with cameras?!

We were shown into a classic bourgeois-rustic dining-room: red brick wallpaper, open stonework, one big dresser with flowery plates, and windows small enough to prevent anyone looking in and discovering there's actually a restaurant in there. The menu was classically Burgundian, and I was tempted by Madame Losset to try the *rognons de veau sauce moutarde*. I have been perenially queasy about kidneys. And here, in this land of Christian monasteries, came my conversion. The meat was sweet and tender, and the cream and wine sauce with tiny mushrooms had the merest hint of mustard. Not over-rich, almost delicate. It was perfectly accompanied by a light 1987 red burgundy at its three-year-old best, brom Bertrand Chezeaux at Nuits.

After lunch, we ask the reticent Monsieur Losset if he will let us quote the recipe in this book. Surprise, surprise: he agrees. He is sweating profusely, though, and disappears into the kitchen. Madame Losset is astonished: '*Normalement*, he is terrified of publicity'. When he returns we expect to see a written recipe in his hand. But no. He wags his head, wiping the sweat off his face with a dishcloth. '*Ça ne m'intéresse pas!*' he apologizes.

What had made him change his mind – on the verge of letting us into his secrets? It remained a mystery. We left, on the best of terms, strangely happy that a bastion of true French gastronomy had been preserved. But we were in trouble. Would all Burgundians be so secretive? In fact, it was rare. And things began to look up with Christiane Gutigny.

We checked into the comfortable Bed-and-Breakfast she runs with her husband, Paul, for three nights and stayed for two weeks. In the lushly wooded hills of the Hautes-Côtes de Nuits, the Gutignys built a modern villa with the proceeds of a farm sold for three times what they paid for it. Apart from the B & B, Christine has a budding ragtrade business, making dresses to order in the garage; Paul keeps sheep, chickens and 'butterfly' rabbits. They exude energy, proof of the old adage: if you want something done, ask a busy Burgundian. Christiane, whose Auxerrois mother cooked for a Parisian banker, found time to pass on some of her family knowledge to us.

To the layman, the wine sauce called

Oeufs en meurette

meurette, with lardons, baby onions and button mushrooms, always has eggy associations. In fact, its origins were fishy – the word meant a freshwater fish stew (*matelote*) of eel, carp and tench made with red wine.

As Paul Gutigny brought in a dozen fresh eggs from his hens, Christiane was getting down to business with the calmness of a true cook and chatting non-stop about something entirely different – Burgundian nicknames: '. . . and a man

with false teeth is called *le bavoud* because he dribbles. A man who kills pigs is *le sauce*, short for saucisson.'

Christiane often burnt the breakfast toast, talking too much. We wondered how her *oeufs en meurette* would fare, but an aroma of hot wine and onions soon filled the kitchen. It was a house of smells for all seasons: jams and blackcurrant juice in summer, *meurette* in winter.

One of Paul's rabbits became *lapin à la moutarde*. For the best mustard sauce, you must have the best mustard. And it doesn't come better than from Fallot.

The house of Fallot, in a picturebook nineteenth-century factory at Beaune, make mustards with wine or vinegar or *verjus* (juice of unripe white grapes), with tarragon or spices. The yellow fields we had seen everywhere were colza, not mustard; today's mustard seeds come from Canada. There are too many vineyards and no fields big enough for the prairie crop.

Our eyes were stinging, tears pouring down our faces, not from the demise of the Burgundian mustard seed but from the very potent Canadian ones being crushed in the millstones.

Without Dijon mustard, a Burgundian

*Right: Mural
at Fallot's
mustard
factory,
Beaune*

andouillette is just another tripe sausage – even from a butcher like Mornard who makes the best in Mâcon. They are a local passion. Colette Morel, a rare female wine-maker in charge of restaurateur Georges Blanc's Domaine d'Azenay, says gaily: 'To hell with diets! My favourite dish is *andouillette à la mâconnaise*. You just cover the sausage with mustard and butter, put a little white Mâcon in the dish and bake in the oven. Before serving, pour over some cream. What could be easier than that?'

It is easier still to be confused by the names of regional dishes and sauces. What is the difference between *à la nivernaise* and *sauce nivernaise*?

Pierre Langlois is chef of the Restaurant de la Poste, Varzy, a little town tucked away in the poorest of Burgundy's departments, the Nièvre, surrounded by that empty, dormant countryside of woodland and prairie known as *la France profonde*.

'Sauce nivernaise is made with white wine, garlic, butter and shallots,' Pierre told us. 'Delicious with raw vegetables like fennel, cauliflower or celery. Whereas *à la nivernaise* is meat accompanied by carrots, onions and braised lettuce – a

Grey-Poupon
mustard shop,
Dijon

way of cooking rather than a sauce.'

Nor is *à la morvandelle* a sauce. This just means a cooked dish containing Morvan ham. Even *à la mâconnaise* should not strictly be applied to the mustard sauce for an *andouillette*; according to *Larousse Gastronomique* it is a way of cooking fish in herbs and red wine, accompanied by baby onions, croûtons and crayfish.

The natives use their terms loosely. Sometimes it's inevitable. Even Pierre has been known to improvise, especially when travelling the world in the cause of French gastronomy. As chef in charge of promoting Burgundian dishes in Zimbabwe and unable to find Charolais beef in Africa, he saved the day successfully with his *impala à la nivernaise*.

Among other Burgundian sauce wizards was a Dijon widow, Madeleine Lecat. Her mother once owned seven farms, and she was brought up on the best of country cooking. Only later did she learn to cook - out of necessity. Her father was killed in World War I, then her husband in World War II, and late in life she became a secretary to support her family. Compiled over the years, her private recipe book is a tome of culinary wisdom, including a simple way of livening up leftovers of your joint with *sauce ravigote*.

Dijon mustard window display

Mâcon andouillettes – tripe sausages from Boucherie Mornand

Useful tips about sauces also came from Armand Poinsot of Chez Camille, Arnay-le-Duc: 'Avoid *beurre-manié* (butter and flour) for thickening a sauce. It's indigestible. Use just flour and water.'

Patrick Gatinet at the Hotel-Restaurant de la Tour, bringing much-needed life and style to a dull suburb of Mâcon, showed us how to perk up a red or white wine sauce just before serving, a trick called *la tombée du dernier moment*. 'Stir in a glass of wine from the bottle at the last moment,' he demonstrated. 'That's my recipe for happiness!' It certainly did wonders for his *côte de boeuf charolais au sauce marchand*.

We were intrigued by his portrait of a spry old man in a rakish hat. 'Ah, Jean Dubois,' Patrick told us. 'One hundred and two this year. A true Rablelaisian. He even addresses me as *tavernier*. He was still chasing women at 85 and regularly drank four litres of Mâcon-Viré a day. He's attended the funerals of four family doctors. The fifth is understandably nervous.'

I should add that Monsier Dubois has never smoked or drunk hard liquor. But what a testimony to Burgundy's wine and sauces!

Left: Pernand-Vergelesses – Côte de Beaune wine-making village

LAPIN À LA MOUTARDE

Rabbit in mustard and white wine sauce. Even in Burgundy the wine drunk and the wine cooked with, may not be the same colour, let alone from the same bottle. I suggest a 1978 Pernard-Vergelesses Grand Cru from Girard-Vollot at Savigny-lès-Beaune to drink with this. Recipe of Christiane Gutigy. Serves 5.

1 rabbit, weighing about 4½ lb/2kg
sunflower oil or other vegetable oil
½ oz/15g (1 tbs) unsalted butter
2 tbs flour
1 large onion, coarsely chopped
at least 1 clove garlic, more to taste,
finely chopped
bouquet garni of fresh thyme, parsley
and bay leaf
1 bottle white burgundy
3 tbs Dijon mustard
3 egg yolks
8fl oz/250ml (1 cup) double (heavy)
cream
salt, pepper

Cut the rabbit into pieces, or have the butcher do it for you.

Brown the rabbit pieces on all sides in the sunflower oil in a large frying pan (skillet) or flameproof casserole. Set aside.

Make a roux by melting the butter and stirring in the flour, then stir over medium heat for about 2 minutes. Add the onion, garlic and bouquet garni, then stir in the wine. Continue stirring until smooth. Season to taste.

Add the rabbit pieces. Simmer covered, over medium heat until the rabbit is tender, up to 1 hour.

Beat together the mustard, egg yolks and cream. About 5 minutes before serving, stir the mustard mixture into the pan and warm through.

Season to taste. Transfer to a heated platter and serve.

CÔTE DE BOEUF CHAROLAIS AU SAUCE MARCHAND

A simple Burgundian classic of grilled Charolais beef in a shallot-and-red-wine sauce. Use the same wine for cooking and drinking: a fat and deep-red 1989 Macon-Igé from the Igé co-operative is just right for the beef. Recipe of Patrick Gatinet. Serves 2.

1 rib of beef on the bone, generous
1½ lb/750g
FOR THE MARINADE
dash of Cognan
fresh thyme
1 bay leaf
salt, freshly-milled white pepper
FOR THE SAUCE
4 shallots, finely chopped
1 wine glass red-wine vinegar
2 wine glasses red wine
8fl oz/250 ml (1 cup) beef stock
freshly-milled white pepper

Combine the marinade ingredients, then marinate the beef for 1 hour.

Meanwhile, make the sauce. Simmer the shallots and vinegar until all the liquid has been absorbed by the shallots. Deglaze with 1 wine glass of red wine. Add the stock, then simmer until reduced and thickened. Keep warm.

Grill, fry or barbecue the beef according to taste (two of you, remember!). When ready to serve, pour the second glass of wine into the sauce and give a twist of the pepper-mill over it. Serve the sauce on the side.

Pont d'Ouche – port on Canal de Bourgogne

SAUCE
BOURGUIGNONNE
POUR POISSONS

*Clos de
Vougeot – Côte
de Nuits
vineyard for
top red
burgundy*

This classic sauce is served with freshwater fish from the Saône or Loire, such as eel. perch, pike or trout. Serves 4–6.

*bones and trimmings of 1 fish
1¾ pints / 1 litre (4½ cups) red
burgundy*

*1 onion, finely chopped
small bouquet garni of thyme, parsley
and bay leaf
1 handful finely chopped
mushrooms
salt, pepper
1oz/30g (2 tbs) butter
1 tb flour*

Bring all the ingredients, except the butter and flour, to a boil, then simmer for 30 minutes. Strain and reserve the stock, and use the back of a large wooden spoon to push as much as possible of the solid ingredients through the sieve. Simmer for 10 minutes, until the liquid is reduced by half.

Thicken with the flour and butter mixed into a *beurre-manié*, or follow Armand Poinsot's advice and make it with water and flour: add 2 tbs water to 1½ tbs flour. If the sauce is not thick enough for your taste, thicken again with another *beurre-manié*.

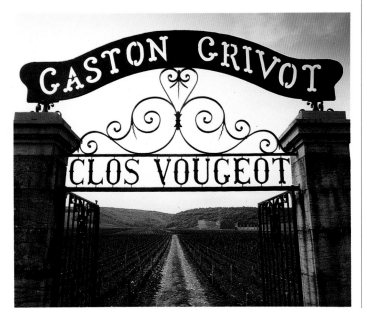

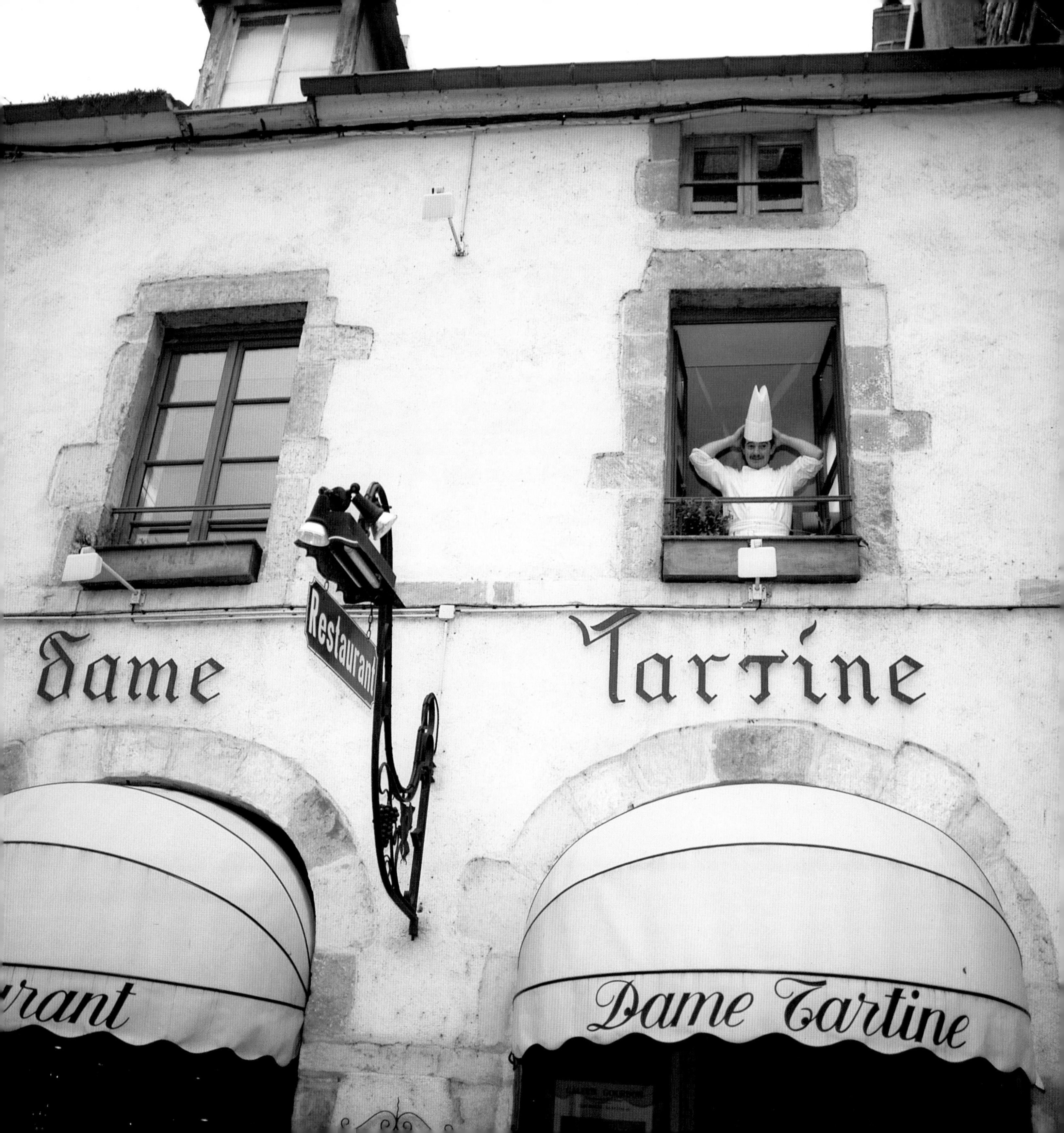
Restaurant
Dame Tartine
...urant
Dame Tartine

SAUCE RAVIGOTE

I treasure this simple recipe, a useful sauce to jolly up the remains of a roast of lamb or veal. *Les restes* (leftovers) are one of the goodliest morsels of French cooking. Recipe of Madeleine Lecat. Serves 4.

> *leftover meat (see above)*
> *flour for sprinkling meat*
> *butter or oil for sautéing*
> *½ wine glass dry white burgundy*
> *(Aligoté, Pouilly-Fumé)*
> *1 tsp vinegar*
> *1 sprig fresh parsley, finely chopped*
> *2 shallots, chopped*

Cut the meat into small pieces, then sprinkle with the flour. Heat the butter or oil in a heavy-based frying pan (skillet) and sauté the meat until it is golden, stirring constantly.

Add a little water, the wine and vinegar and stir well. Leave to simmer for 5 minutes.

Sprinkle with the parsley and shallots mixed together just before serving.

OEUFS EN MEURETTE

Eggs poached in a red wine and onion sauce. Madame Gutingy says: 'The more you keep heating the sauce up and letting it cool, the better it is. It can be made the day before. Drink the cheapest good-quality burgundy you can find to make the dish with: a Passe-Tout-Grains (one third Pinot, two-thirds Gamay) from a reliable maker. Recipe of Christiane Gutigny. Serves 4.

> *8 rashers (slices) bacon, cubed*
> *2oz/50g (¼ cup) butter*
> *2 tbs olive oil or vegetable oil*
> *4 med onions, roughly chopped*
> *2 cloves garlic (1 reserved;*
> *1 chopped)*
> *2 tbs plain flour*
> *1 bottle red burgundy*
> *bouquet garni of fresh thyme, parsley*
> *and bay leaf*
> *8 slices French bread*
> *8 eggs*
> *salt, pepper*

Fry the bacon in the melted butter and oil, then remove with a slotted spoon and set aside. Brown the onions and chopped garlic in the same oil.

Sprinkle the flour over the onions and stir to make a roux. Stir in the wine and bring to the boil. Set alight to remove the wine's acidity and alcohol, then add the bouquet garni and simmer, coverer for 3 hours. When you are almost ready to serve, toast the bread, then rub with the reserved garlic clove. About 3 minutes before serving, poach the eggs into the *meurette* sauce. Season (not too much salt because of the bacon cubes). Transfer the eggs to a hot serving dish, surrounded by the fried bacon cubes and garlic toast. Serve at once.

CANON KIR

I drink for the thirst to come.

RABELAIS

'One gets drunk too quickly on a *vin blanc cassis*,' declared our host, Antoine Cornu.

He should know. *Bon viveur*, a large man in heart and body, Antoine is a widower, retired oil executive living in a fine house in the suburbs of Dijon, Burgundy's capital and birthplace of the *vin blanc cassis*, otherwise known as kir. Native of Chalon-sur-Saône, his R's had a rich, Burgundian roll to them, like those of Colette who was born at Sauveur-en-Puisaye.

Long before Antoine and Colette, the original Burgundes tribes came from the German Baltic in the fifth century. It is even possible they brought blackcurrants with them, for *cassis* is essentially a northern fruit.

Antoine replenished our glasses with just the right one-third of *crème de cassis*, the blackcurrant liqueur with a potent eighteen degrees of alcohol, and topped it up, surprisingly, with two-thirds red burgundy. 'That's a *Communard*,' he laughed. Made with red wine, it is less intoxicating than with white for some mysterious oenological reason.

The origin of kir, he told us, was a comparatively recent legend. Canon Kir was a well-loved Resistance hero. When he became mayor of Dijon, he always served white wine and *cassis* at the *Hôtel de Ville*; in the Sixties the name caught on and made him world famous.

On the upper slopes of the Côte d'Or, known as the Hautes Côtes, are fields of blackcurrants among the vineyards. Arguably the best *crème de cassis* is made at Arcenant by Gilles Joannet, *liquoriste*. His is a backyard industry, the making of the liqueurs carried out in a chaotic shed which looks more like a poteen still in County Cork. Gilles is a soft-spoken bear of a man with a wicked twinkle. When the postman refused a drink, Gilles teased: 'It's because of these English. If they put you in their book drinking with me, you'd lose your job.'

Blackcurrants are harvested in July. Gilles has eight hectares on chalky, stony, south-facing slopes. Whatever terrain vines like, so do blackcurrants – only higher. After pulping, 130 litres of alcohol are added to 1200 kilos of fruit. Ninety days later, the juice is removed. Gilles continues to press until the skins yield their last drop, with the whole shambly shed giving off a heady aroma of blackcurrant. I asked how you could tell a well-made *crème de cassis*. 'Upend the bottle, and stand it straight again,' he said. 'If the top of the bottle stays purple, the liqueur is good.'

Aubert and Pamela de Villaine in their Bouzeron Aligoté vineyard

He also warned us that even the best *crème de cassis* only keeps a year, unlike the white wine that goes with it. Traditionally, the wine is made from Aligoté, a grape grown on land which will take neither Pinot, from which nearly all red burgundies are made, nor Chardonnay, which is the grape for most of the region's whites.

'What?!' exclaimed wine-maker Aubert de Villaine. 'You put Bouzeron Aligoté in a photograph of a kir?'

He sounded quite indignant, and I took it to be due to the hour. Aubert and his Pasadena-born wife, Pamela, had kindly agreed to show us their vineyard at 8.30 in the morning. Mayor of the tiny village of Bouzeron at the head of a lost, romantic valley, Aubert had municipal duties later that morning. But what had we done wrong?

This erudite, aristocratic figure, son of a French banker and a Russian mother, was hardly intimidating. 'Bouzeron Aligoté became an *appellation contrôllé* in 1979,' he explained. Aubert had fought a crusade for that *appellation*, and indeed Bouzeron is the best Aligoté, deliciously dry, a little green. 'I'm trying to get it drunk as a wine on its own – either as an aperitif or with *fruits de mer*.'

*Alain
Geoffroy,
Chablis
winemaker,
tasting in his
cellar*

From the cosy sitting room of their village house, decorated with china dogs and prints, Aubert and Pamela took us to the vineyard. It had a primeval feeling: undersea fossils dating from prehistory were found there and a ruined medieval chapel gives the parcel its name, L'Hermitage. Aubert likes the sense of continuity, and resembled a monastic hermit himself as he bent to examine a young, sprouting vine.

Aperitif white wines are legion in Burgundy. I was offered a Meursault 'Les Gouttes d'Or' Premier Cru by capon-farmer Jean-Pierre Quignard, for elevenses; his wife, Madeleine, mistakenly believing it to be Aligoté, pushed the *crème de cassis* across the kitchen table, and received a ribald rebuke. It was very *typé*, everyone agreed, the greenest, most aggressive young Meursault imaginable with lots of juniper about it. After ten minutes' drinking with cured ham and farmhouse bread, however, it had lost its aggressivity and was almost mellow.

Alain Geoffroy, who won an award in 1991 for his renowned Domaine le Verger Chablis, has three 'first-growth' vineyards near the Lac de Beine, where fishermen spend peaceful hours while he's faxing England, Japan and Germany. Seventy per cent of his business is export. He gave us a tasting in his cellar: 'Vau Ligneau' was lightest, very aromatic; 'Beauroy' more marked, full-bodied, longer in mouth; 'Fourchaume, voluptuous, tenderer, even longer in the mouth. 'If you can afford it,' our host said laconically, 'a first-growth Chablis makes a good *apéro*.' I'd settle for 'Vau Ligneau' any day – perhaps with a slither of country ham.

Not far from Chablis, in Burgundy's most northerly department of the Yonne, are lesser-known, less-expensive wines of increasing quality – the light Irancy red; Épineuil all three colours; and Vézelay, an

Mid-morning Meursault tasting with chicken farmer Jean-Pierre Quignard

Caves de Bailly's underground cellars

upcoming dry white from a vineyard only reclaimed in 1986 but now good enough to be served by Marc Meneau, another of the Burgundy Big Six chefs, at L'Espérance. Good *apéros*, all.

Most spectacular of the northern pre-meal wines is a *Crémant de Bourgogne* from the *Caves de Bailly*. 'Crémant' means creaming, and expresses the semi-sparkling froth of the wine as it rises in your glass when poured. They do not put *méthode champenoise* on their bottles, because their vinification is not just a champagne 'method', it is precisely the same as that used in Épernay. And a good *Crémant de Bourgogne* is a much better party buy than a supermarket 'Champlonk' – at half the price.

Penetrating a stark cliff overlooking the weeping willows of the River Yonne, the Caves de Bailly form an awe-inspiring, three-hectare Aladdin's cave of five million *crémant* bottles, white and rosé. It was a twelfth-century quarry from which came the stone that built Notre-Dame in Paris. Fifty-five metres below ground, conditions are just right for storage: no vibration, a constant 12°C, which is ideal for the froth.

At a stage-set bar carved out of the cavernous rock and open to the public, we were entertained by Monsieur Guérard. 'The English prefer our rosé as an *apéro*,' he said. 'But it's also good with dessert. Drink the white with fish, the demi-sec with foie gras . . .' We steered him back to *apéros*. 'Well, there's no Canon of Auxerre, so we have to call our white with *crème de cassis* a kir royal.'

I preferred less pretentious mixes. Caves de Bailly also make their own liqueurs. Ratafia, the *vigneron*'s aperitif made from grape must (skins and stalks after pressing) and *eau-de-vie*. And the fruit liqueurs: cherry from the famous Auxerrois crop, peach, and blackberry. Mixed exactly like a kir were blackberry topped up with white *crémant*, cherry with Irancy red, and peach with an Épineuil rosé.

Paradoxically, with all their fine wines, Burgundians love cocktails. Also made with the local fizz, Marc Millot's was accompanied by an unusual *amuse-gueule* ('palate-tickler') of chicken wings with mushrooms in beetroot juice.

Burgundian apertifs greatly outnumber the *amuse-gueule* choice. With a St-Véran white, we had tiny goat's cheeses called *boutons de culotte* (trouser buttons) at Mâcon. And there was always the delicious ham. But the regular standby of winetasters is the famous *gougère* – a cheese puff soft on the inside and crispy brown on the outside.

Queen of the *gougère* is Marie-Thérèse Bazeron at her Beaune *patisserie*. 'I was born in this house,' she told us. 'My family owned it for more than a hundred years. How can the kids know what shops were like when there were real shopkeepers? Mine is a museum.'

She puts her eye to the spyhole in a Lalique glass partition that separates her shabby back premises from the 'museum'. The steady stream of Sunday regulars make it too crowded to sit at the marble-top tables or see the time by the ormolu clock. It has stopped, anyway – like all time chez Bazeron.

Marie-Thérèse Bazeron (on left) in her Beaune patisserie

GOUGÈRE

A cheese puff accompaniment to wine tastings or aperitifs. It can be eaten warm or cold, but preferably on the day of making. Recipe of Marie-Thérèse Bazeron. Serves 6.

12fl oz/350ml (1½ cups) water
4oz/125g (½ cup) butter
salt, pepper
8oz/250g (2 cups) flour
5–6 eggs, according to size
7oz/200g Gruyere cheese, cut into
thin strips or coarsely grated
extra butter for greasing baking tray
(cookie sheet)
1 egg, beaten

Bring the water, butter and a pinch of salt to the boil. Remove from the heat, then add all the flour at once. Beat well with a wooden spoon, then return to heat and continue beating until the pastry forms a ball and comes away from the sides of the pan, 2–3 minutes.

Remove from the heat again. Add the eggs, 1 at a time, making sure each is fully incorporated before adding another. Stir in the Gruyère. Add a little salt (not too much because of the cheese) and pepper.

Place on a buttered baking tray (cookie sheet) in small balls, not too close together. Brush with the beaten egg and bake at 350°F/180°C/Gas Mark 5 for 40 minutes, until puffed and golden.

COCKTAIL D'HYDROMEL

A mead cocktail made with *Crémant de Bourgogne*. Recipe of Marc Millot. Makes 1.

In a champagne flute, mix 3½fl oz/100ml (scant ½ cup) mead with 2fl oz/60 ml (¼ cup) Grand Marnier. Top with *Crémant de Bourgogne*. Garnish with a cherry (preferable preserved in brandy).

OTHER APERITIFS

WHITE WINES

Bouzeron Aligoté: Dry, fruity, green and best drunk young.

Vézelay: An upcoming northern Chardonnay.

Mâcon-Villages: Typical *Chardonnay* of southern Burgundy.

St-Véran: The same rich style as Pouilly-Fuissé but better value for money.

Pouilly Fumé: A Loire Sauvignon, pale and flinty.

Chablis: Golden, subtle and strictly for treats.

Meursault: A classic mellow wine, but be careful where you buy it.

Puligny-Montrachet: Rich, dry and very expensive. (The middle "t" is silent.)

RED AND ROSÉ WINES

Bourgogne Rouge: A plain red Pinot Noir. Variable quality.

Hautes-Côtes de Nuits: An upcoming lightish red, best drunk young.

Épineuil: Light and fruity, red and rosé are produced.

Mâcon: A Gamay a little heavier than neighbouring Beaujolais.

FIZZY WINES

Crémant de Bourgogne

FRUIT AND WINE COMBINATIONS

These are classically made of one-third fruit liqueur to two-thirds wine. Personally, I prefer them less fruity: one-quarter fruit liqueur to three-quarters wine.

Kir: Aligoté white with blackcurrant

Communard: Red burgundy with blackcurrant

Kir royal: Crémant de Bourgogne with blackcurrant

Irancy red with cherry

Crémant de Bourgogne with blackberry

Épineuil rosé with peach

HOME GROWN AND WILD

Oulon, with its sweet, calm fishing pond could normally claim to be the Nièvre's quietest village. Sunday midday at the Auberge du Vieux Château, however, the whole department seemed to have descended on it. Cars jammed the court-yard, men were playing *boules,* children cavorted in the swimming pool and the last lunch guests did not leave the turret-ed house until 7.30 pm. It was a tribute to the cooking of Christiane Fayolle, aided by her daughter Catherine.

Everything we ate during our stay at this *table d'hôte* (guest house with all meals available) was from the farm. Besides charcuterie from home-grown pigs, there were super-fresh starters like a red lettuce salad of duck's gizzards, green beans sprinkled with parsley and garlic, a goat's cheese salad. House wine was ner-vous young Coteaux du Giennois VDQS from the banks of the nearby Loire, which divides Burgundy from Berry.

The Nièvre's comparative poverty stems from its lack of vineyards, com-pared to the other Burgundian depart-ments (Yonne, Côte d'Or, Saône-et-Loire). My hot goat's cheese deserved a better wine: perhaps a white St-Véran from La Domaine des Deux-Roches, Davayé. Jean-Luc Terrier, his father and two brothers make some of the best wine in the Mâconnais, holding their own against their grander neighbour, Pouilly-Fuissé, which the innocent abroad can never find because the *appellation* is actu-ally two villages, Pouilly and Fuissé.

Jean-Luc showed us 'Les Terres Noires' vineyard, so called because its soil has more stones than earth which, though scarce, is particularly rich in black leaf mould. That and the sheltered, south-fac-ing slopes make it ideal for producing St-Véran. Kept in oak barrels for six months, it is ready to drink a year after bottling.

A note of caution: you can drink wine with a goat's cheese salad because, ideally, it's made with hazelnut oil. Any salad

The Nivernais countryside from La Butte de Montemoison

rolling, hedgeless prairies west of Tonnerre, where vinification takes place. 'There's never a dull moment,' said François. 'In summer and autumn it's one harvest after another.' His 1989 rosé, fresh and full of fruit, won a Gault-Millau award for the best Épineuil in a blind-tasting of 700 reds, whites and rosés.

It was his wine that accompanied a miracle of a starter from New Burgundian Christophe Cussac, chef of L'Abbaye St-Michel at nearby Tonnerre. His *fondant de foies blonds aux pommes vinaigrées* was a chicken liver mousse, showing the young chef's penchant for use of spices like coriander, curry and *quatre épices* (mixed ground cinnamon, ginger, clove and nutmeg).

Chicken livers were closer to the accepted idea of 'delicatessen'. But the Burgundian speciality is strictly non-kosher – ham of all kinds from simple *jambon blanc* (cooked ham) to more complex *jambon sec à la lie de vin*. This is smoked and dried ham macerated in lees – the deposit left in oak barrels after fine wine has been removed. And lucky restaurateurs like the Poinsots, of Chez Camille at Arnay-le-Duc, cure their own ham on the home farm. 'We must be

with vinegar means wine is wasted; one kills the other on the palate. A Terrier Mâcon-Villages, fresh, dry and perfumed, would go better with a charcuterie starter – rillettes or pâté.

Another wine-maker, François Collin, also recommends his Épineuil *rosé* with what he quaintly calls 'delicatessen products' (charcuterie starters of ham, sausage and pâté) in his brochure. And very good it is, too.

François is one of the rare Burgundian farmers making a go of poly-culture. His grapes are transported from the micro-climate slopes of Épineuil to his vast, windswept cereal farm in the middle of

Left: Gill Vié and his mother Andrée at their Nuits St-Georges shop

'crazy,' said Monique Poinsot philosophically. 'Buying two farms – one to live in, one for the restaurant. We'll be in debt forever.'

Madame Poinsot was hardly dressed for farming. In shiny wellingtons, white silk shirt with pearls, a *soignée* padded jacket with glittering brooch, sleek black hair perfectly coiffed, she sludged about in manure and pig shit. But the huge Landrasse porkers were as pristine as Madame – almost pets to the farm children, Virginie and Alexis, who chased them with a mixture of terror and cries of glee. They hated it when a pig had to turn into sausages or become *jambon persillé à l'Aligoté* on the Chez Camille menu.

Dijon claims to be the originator of this celebrated galantine of ham and parsley starter, but we found it everywhere. Champions of its cause were butcher Régis Vié, wife Andrée and son Gill at their fourth generation shop in Nuits-St-Georges. The shop has medieval stained-glass panels showing the nearby monastery at Clos de Vougeot, the birth of Jesus, and the killing of the pascal lamb.

'Yet in Burgundy, ham, not lamb, was traditionally eaten at Easter,' explained Madame Vié – grey-haired, birdlike and inclined to pick up the wrong knife to carve the ham. 'With *jambon persillé* the pink of the ham and the green of the parsley suggest spring flowers and budding vines.'

Working like a mad scientist at some fiendish experiment, a professional *jambon persillé* maker shreds huge steaming hams, hurls garlic and shallot purées into the pot, sprinkles secret spices, sherry and wine vinegars, ladels and stirs until you're invited to taste the mixture. 'Not enough garlic!' someone comments. 'More spice!' says another. Back to work goes the mad scientist, mumbling incantations to himself. 'Please,' he says turning to you nervously. 'You will not reveal my secret, will you?' He needn't worry: his wild concocting has all gone much too fast for you to detect that *je-ne-sais-quoi*, that subtle spice that makes his *jambon persillé* quite the best in Burgundy. If possible, made with Morvan ham.

Bob Waggoner has a special predeliction for Morvan ham. The Californian chef knows Burgundy well by now. From LA's Trumps restaurant, he came to France under the auspices of the helpful New York wine-broker Becky

Chef Bob Waggoner and his wife Christine at Le Monte Cristo, Moneteau

Right: Auberge des Amognes, Montigny aux Amognes, near Nevers

opened in 1990, it is already on the up. 'We need more businessmen at lunch, though,' Bob said. At night, all the tables with their beautiful china – Bob's passion – were full.

A little more basic than Bob's sumptuous Morvan ham salad, is a traditional *nivernais* ham starter we found at one of the rare, genuine country inns, the Auberge des Amognes, Montigny aux Amognes. 'I hate flat, international French cuisine, fussed up with herbs and spices,' said Paul Bélujon. His wife, Raymonde, is a painter but the decor was refreshingly trad: copper warming pans, grandfather clock, oxen yoke, stuffed foxes and antlers, blue and white chequed napkins in a fan shape.

'The Nièvre once had a great *cuisine du terroir*,' Paul told us. 'In the days of our beef, Nivernais chefs would be popular in Paris – just as the best barmen would be Auvergnats. Nowadays . . .' He wagged his head sadly. 'Most tucked-away country auberges can't make it. Thank God we have the city of Nevers only twelve kilometres away.'

The citizens of Nevers are lucky to have the Bélujon *saupiquet nivernais* so close.

Wasserman, now based in Bouilland. It was at that village's Hostellerie du Vieux-Moulin he began 'seriously cooking'. After stints with top chefs Silva, Lameloise and Meneau, he married Christine, a receptionist at the Hotel de la Poste, Avallon, and together they bought a bourgeois Moneteau house with private park to start their own restaurant. Only

Market outside St-Vincent cathedral, Chalon-sur-Saône

If the Nièvre is short on country inns, it is rich in trees. The pine and oak woods cover more surface than its fields; it is the most afforested department in France. 'Our wealth is in the forests,' claims Pierre Langlois.

For his Varzy restaurant, Pierre has perfected the blanching and deep-freezing of wild mushrooms. He swears it totally preserves their freshness. And to judge by his *fricassée de champignons*, he is ahead of the game. On our plates was a mixture of *chanterelles* (orange becoming chestnut when cooked), *trompettes des morts* (black) and *ceps* (grey), sprinkled with chives, shallots, garlic and chervil.

'Into the woods!' around Varzy has no sinister portent. For Pierre, it means making some culinary discovery, finding a plant or herb long forgotten – with the same innocent enthusiasm as Colette, born at St-Sauveur-en-Puisaye, who went looking for water chestnuts as a young girl. 'That's how *cuisine de terroir* can remain a very French thing,' Pierre reckons. 'Long ago, I discovered wild asparagus. My Parisian colleagues were impressed. We country cooks are often avante-garde with produce that afterwards becomes à la mode!'

From countryside to top restaurant, the produce makes its progress – via the popular markets like Chalon-sur-Saône, where chefs drive thirty miles or more each week to make their dawn purchases. At the bar opposite the cathedral of St-Vincent-des-Prés, elbows are raised by the star chefs and the upcoming ones – those with a red 'R' in the Michelin Guide

Pierre Langlois' fricassé de champignons

for their excellent quality price ratio. A quick *casse-croûte* (bar snack), a glass of *mâconnais*, and it's home, home to the range with the *camionnette* stuffed with fruit and vegetables and crayfish fresh from the nearby Saône.

'Caught this morning by a fisherman friend,' Jacques Lainé informed us, as a sophisticated starter *flan d'écrivisses* appeared in the elegant, flower-filled, Napoléon III dining-room of his Beaune restaurant. In the kitchen crayfish had clung fiercely to his fingers; now they were laid peacefully to rest among the tiny stems of wild asparagus.

It was the asparagus season. And the dishes were getting further and further from the woods. In the village of Bouilland is the Hostellerie du Vieux-Moulin, presided over by young New Burgundian, Jean-Pierre Silva and his wife, Isabelle (whose name comes first on the menu cover, a chivalrous habit of most married chefs).

Don't let the designer decor of painted mill-wheel, birds-of-paradise, halogen lighting and a Japanese water-garden fool you. Jean-Pierre, whatever elaborate decor and dishes he may invent, is a staunch upholder of Burgundian tradition – like a modern ballet choreographer rethinking classical steps. 'I do variations on traditional themes, mixing unusual things together,' he told us. 'When I travel, I always go native in my eating. I get some of my most elaborate ideas in the simplest restaurants, sniffing pots and asking what's in them. From Guadeloupe,

for example, I got the idea of doing a John Dory fish poached in coconut milk with mango.'

When I pointed out not one element of that dish was Burgundian, Jean-Pierre laughed: 'And even I'm Lyonnais. One has to be outward-looking and inventive. But I'm passionate for local produce, I promise you. Most of my ingredients come from within forty kilometres.' The use of local ingredients was also true for the vegetables in our appetizers of *assiette de legumes du moment au bouillon de jambon, quelques gouttes d'huile de noisette* (baby vegetables – carrots, onions, mange-tout – in a ham stock with a dash of hazelnut oil) and *ragoût d'asperges et premières morilles printanières* (ragout of asparagus and early spring morels).

Just as my head was reeling from the fashionably long dish titles on the menu, Isabelle Silva came in with some down-to-earth common sense about the wine we'd been drinking before the meal – a white Pernand-Vergelesses Premier Cru. 'I like it,' she said. 'There's only two things that matter about wine – I like it, I don't like it – everything else is of secondary importance.' Nothing chichi about the Silvas.

RAGOÛT D'ASPERGES ET PREMIÈRES MORILLES PRINTANIÈRES

Ragout of asparagus with morel mushrooms (fresh if possible, bottled if not). Monsieur Silva says: 'As the morel is a noble mushroom, it deserves a noble white – a sweet-scented Chevalier-Montrachet or dry and mellow Mersault les Perrières from the upper, sunniest slopes.' Recipe of Jean-Pierre Silva. Serves 4.

40 asparagus spears
14oz/400g morels
8fl oz/250ml (1 cup) chicken stock
8fl oz/250ml (1 cup) soured cream
5oz/150g (²/₃ cup) butter
salt, pepper
4 sprigs fresh chervil, chopped

Trim the asparagus and tie into 4 bundles. Simmer for 10–15 minutes, depending on size, until tender, then immediately cool in cold water. Rinse the morels in cold water; set aside. Put into a flameproof casserole the chicken stock, soured cream, 3½oz/100g (7 tbs) of the butter and salt and pepper. Bring to the boil and continue boiling until reduced by half. Add the morels and simmer for 5–10 minutes, until the cream sauce coats them. Check the seasoning and keep warm. Melt 1½oz/50g of butter in a thick frying pan, arrange the asparagus side by side, season and heat gently.

Meanwhile, warm 4 serving plates. Arrange 10 asparagus spears on each plate. Spoon the morels over the asparagus, then sprinkle with chervil and serve.

FONDANT DE FOIES BLONDS AU POMMES VINAIGRÉES

Chicken liver mousse with spicy potatoes. This invention of New Burgundian Christophe Cussac of L'Abbaye St-Michel, Tonnerre, was enjoyed with a superbly light 1989 red Épineuil from

François Collin. Although the quantity of potatoes looks high, this is the amount the chef says is necessary to get about 1¼ lb/600g good-size rounds. Recipe of Christophe Cussac. Serves 6.

4oz/125g lard
7oz/200g chicken livers, trimmed
1 tsp salt
½ tsp pepper
½ tsp sugar
¼ tsp ground coriander
pinch quatre epices (mixed ground
cinnamon, ginger, clove
and nutmeg)
5⅓oz/160ml (generous ⅔ cup)
double (heavy) cream
3 egg yolks
1⅓ tbs Cognac
¼ pint/150ml (⅔ cup) wine
vinegar
salt, pepper
¼ pint/150ml (⅔ cup) olive oil
2½lb/1kg potatoes, peeled
¾ pint/500ml (2 cups) chicken stock
¼ tsp curry powder
2 tomatoes
2 spring onions (scallions), cut into
julienne strips
10 peppercorns, crushed

Pureé the lard, chicken livers, salt, pepper, sugar, coriander and *quatre epices* in a blender or food processor. Add the cream, eggs yolks and Cognac and process again. Sieve.

Divide the mixture equally between six 5oz/150g (⅔ cup) ramekins lined with cling film (plastic wrap). Place in a roasting tin with enough hot water to come half way up the sides of the ramekins and cook at 250°F/130°C/Gas Mark ½ for 25 minutes. Remove from the water and leave to cool.

Mix the vinegar with salt and pepper, then beat in the olive oil; set aside.

Cut the potatoes into cylinders 1¼ inches/3cm wide, then slice 1¼ inch/3cm thick. Bring the chicken stock to the boil with the curry powder and peppercorns. Add the potatoes and boil for 5 minutes. Meanwhile, plunge the tomatoes into boiling water for 10 seconds, then into cold water. Peel, remove seeds and dice the flesh.

Unmould the mousses onto individual plates. Dress the potatoes with the vinaigrette and surround the mousses with potatoes, tomatoes and onions.

Flan d'Écrevisses

'Flan' is that ubiquitous Latin cooking word that appears in Spanish recipes, too, having nothing to do with pastry. Here it is a mould (no pastry) made with crayfish and garnished with wild asparagus (or asparagus tips) and crayfish shells. Recipe of Jacques Lainé. Serves 4.

40 crayfish
7fl oz/200ml (scant 1 cup) double
(heavy) cream
2 eggs
salt, pepper
2²/₃oz/80g (5¹/₃ tbs) butter, plus extra
for ramekins
fresh chervil sprigs
16 spears wild asparagus or
asparagus tips, cooked

Plunge the crayfish into boiling, salted water until they turn bright red, then remove and leave to cool in cold water.

Shell the tails, reserving 4 good heads for garnishing. Purée the remaining heads, shells and all, in a blender or food processor. Add the cream, eggs and salt and pepper and purée again. Sieve the purée and check the seasoning.

Fill four individual 10oz/300g (1¼ cups) ramekins, reserving the leftover purée. Bake the ramekins in a roasting tin with enough hot water to come up the sides of the ramekins at 300°F/150°C/Gas Mark 2 for 25 minutes.

Meanwhile, place the remaining crayfish purée into a flameproof casserole with a little water and simmer for 10 minutes. Stir in the butter until melted, then sieve the sauce. Taste for seasoning.

Turn out the moulds on to individual plates. Garnish each with a crayfish tail, chervil sprigs and 4 asparagus spears or tips. Pour round the sauce and serve.

SAUPIQUET NIVERNAIS

A simple version of the more elaborate *saupiquet aux amognes*, gammon in a piquant cream sauce. Don't eat this with a Coteaux du Giennois, as we did: it was much too rough and acid. Instead, I suggest you try an Irancy or a young Savigny-lès-Beaune. Recipe of Paul Bélujon. Serves 2.

1 tbs finely chopped shallot
8fl oz/250ml (1 cup) dry white wine
2 large tomatoes
10fl oz/300ml (1¼ cups) double
(heavy) cream
salt, pepper
butter or oil
2 good slices gammon (ham steaks),
½ inch/0.5cm thick

Boil the shallot and wine until reduced by half. Peel the tomatoes, then chop and crush them and add to the shallots. Stir in the cream and season. Simmer 15 minutes over a low heat.

In a large non-stick frying pan (skillet) heat a small amount of butter or oil and fry the gammon on both sides until golden. Put each slice on a warmed plate and spoon over the sauce. Serve at once.

55

JAMBON PERSILLÉ

Galantine of ham and parsley. If you don't want to cook a whole ham, as is traditional, follow the Vié recipe that uses a shoulder of pork instead. Accompany with a Bouzeron Aligoté from Michel Chemorin's Domaine des Corcelles, a crisp, light white for a spring dish. Recipe of the Vié family. Serves 10.

5½–6¾lb/2½–3kg shoulder of pork
on the bone, rind removed but
reserved
1 bunch fresh parsley, chopped
1 head garlic, cloves chopped
2 wine glasses Aligoté burgundy
1 wine glass wine vinegar
2 pinches ground white pepper
FOR THE STOCK
¾ pint/500ml (2 cups) Aligoté
burgundy
2 onions, halved
3 cloves
2 carrots, chopped
2 cloves garlic, peeled
bouquet garni of fresh thyme,
parsley and bay leaf
1 calf's foot
3 pieces of reserved pork rind

To make the stock, put all the ingredients in a large saucepan with ¾ pint/1 litre (4½ cups) water and bring to the boil. Lower the heat and simmer for 50 minutes, skimming as necessary. Strain, reserving all the ingredients.

Simmer the pork in the stock for 3 hours. Remove the pork and de-bone; reserve the stock. Cut the pork into thin, flaky chunks, about 1¼ by ¼ inches/3 by 0.5cm but they can be uneven.

From the reserved stock ingredients, chop the calf's foot meat and the pork rind, as well as the garlic and the parsley. Add the wine and vinegar and season with pepper and mix together.

Pour 2 glasses of stock over the pork pieces. In a china salad bowl, make layers of pork, the chopped meat and parsley mixture and a little stock. Press down each layer well with a saucepan lid. End with a layer of the parsley mixture and put a weight on top. Leave to set for at least 7 hours in the refrigerator.

Jambon du Morvan en Julienne aux Artichauts Accompagnés de Beignets d'Aubergines, Citron Vert et Estragon

Morvan ham salad with artichokes, aubergine (eggplant) fritters, lime and tarragon. This is Bob Waggoner at his New Burgundian best – with surely the longest of the long menu titles currently fashionable. If you can not find Morvan ham, Bayonne or Parma (prosciutto) are acceptable alternatives. Use whatever selection of leaves you have available, as long as the quantity is the same. As there is a dressing (even without vinegar), I think it is best not to drink any wine with this first course salad. Recipe of Bob Waggoner. Serves 4.

7oz/200g oak-leaf lettuce
7oz/200g curly lettuce
3¹/₂oz/100g lamb's lettuce (mâche)
3¹/₂oz/100g purslane
2 artichoke hearts, cooked and sliced
14oz/400g Morvan ham, thinly sliced, fat removed and cut in thin strips

For the Dressing
freshly squeezed juice of 2 limes
8 tbs olive oil
8 tbs groundnut (peanut) oil
2 sprigs fresh tarragon, finely chopped
salt, pepper

For the Fritters
2 eggs
1 ice cube
8 tbs plain flour, plus a little extra oil for deep-frying
8 baby aubergines (eggplants), cut in half

Beat together all the dressing ingredients and set aside. Wash all the leaves, dry and set aside. To make the fritters, mix the eggs with 8fl oz/250ml (1 cup) cold water and the ice cube. Little by little, add the flour but leave some lumps, like curdled milk. Heat the oil in a deep-fat fryer. Roll the aubergine halves in flour, then dip in the batter and fry until golden. On a serving platter, place the mixed leaves, fritters, artichoke hearts and the ham strips in a criss-cross pattern on top. Spoon over the dressing and serve.

SNAIL'S PACE

The discovery of a new dish does more for the human race than the discovery of a new star.
BRILLAT-SAVARIN

A memorable meal in a leisurely manner is one of the pleasures of Burgundy, and we were slowing to the tempo of a snail-hunt. The snail-hunt is the slowest on earth.

The snail season was just beginning, and as the damp weather gave way to warm spring sunshine, the fields and woods would be filling with slow-moving hunters, poking about with sticks for the famous *escargots de Bourgogne*.

Snail-paced, then, was our approach to lunch at the restaurant of Jacques Lameloise, another of Burgundy's Big Six chef's restaurants, in the former railway town of Chagny, where no traveller now goes unless it's to Lameloise.

Nothing so banal as the classic half dozen snails in garlic and parsley butter adorned our starter plate. It was the dish Carey had just photographed: *embeurré d'escargots de Bourgogne aux herbes fraîches*, which came with characteristic gusts of laughter from Jacques. 'We're just getting rid of it on you, so it doesn't go bad,' he joked. 'Snails and a piece of cheese, *ça va?*'

The host's light touch pervaded both cooking and ambience. No solemn temple of gastronomy, this, but an unpretentious smalltown restaurant where families with children and grannies and dogs pack themselves around a big table; glasses are polished seconds before their arrival and yellow roses arranged by Jacques' mother. Tables are so far apart you're not even aware of the other guests, service is so discreet that, when Carey dropped a clean napkin, a waiter had already handed her a fresh one before she could pick it up. Chairs are magicked away as you rise, waiters are soft-spoken but clear as they announce the ingredients and cooking method of each course with pride.

The snails wrapped in cabbage leaves were accompanied by the Lameloise house Chardonnay, deliciously earthy and perfect with snails.

The meal continued its relaxed course: scallops with caviar served on a bed of finely chopped celery, apple, baby marrow and red pepper with a saffron sauce; Bresse chicken with fresh morels; and after the cheese, about ten desserts.

'I like simple things,' Jacques, inventor of *cuisine fraîcheur,* told us. Simple?! 'Not too prepared, I mean – not more than three flavours mixed. The success of a dish is how you cosset it while it cooks, how you season it, how good it looks on the plate. I'm never satisfied. I always feel I can do better.'

The humble snail was in inventive hands. Jacques, although third generation in the family's sixteenth-century Relais de Poste, is every centimetre a New Burgundian. Traditional, over-rich sauces are unnecessary nowadays, he thinks; before refrigeration, they were a means of preservation, as were *confits.* Transportation, also, had revolutionized regional cuisine; Burgundian cooking was evolving with new products. Fish arrived fresh from the sea, peppers and aubergines from the Midi.

And some elements even came from abroad. Sssssh! No, no, not . . . SNAILS?!

Chez Billot, in Bassou, we were let into a secret not as shameful as it seems. Loïc Gallois, whose card says 'Quality Manager', was clad like us in regulation white coats and gumboots, to take us round this deep-country, flower-covered eighteenth-century snail factory which is more hygienic than many a hospital. He explained the Burgundian snail's gradual disappearance: 'Hedges have gone with prairie farming, gardeners use chemical fertilizer on their lettuces and make land inhospitable. So where is a poor snail to breed?'

Originally one of the three edible snail species (out of 450), the snail of Burgundy was known as *escargot des vignes* but with the pesticides used by today's wine-makers, a snail wouldn't be seen dead in a vineyard. Or rather, would.

'So', said Monsieur Gallois resignedly, 'our *escargots de Bourgogne* come from Germany, Poland, Hungary and Bulgaria.'

The problem is to preserve the organoleptic quality, so a deep-frozen snail excites the taste-buds – and safely. Anyone who has had food poisoning from a dodgy snail, as I have, will be grateful for the care with which the Billot factory prepares its product.

Right: Hotel-Restaurant of Jacques Lameloise, one of Burgundy's 'Big Six' chefs, Chagny

Heating up snails at the Billot factory, Bassou

For the pre-Christmas rush, steaming cauldrons were unfreezing the snails which arrive in blocks. The shells come separately in cartons. Two hundred women were checking every shell, every snail for the slightest fault. The snails were then put back home in their shells and moved to another department where parsley-and-garlic butter was added. Then they were again deep frozen by a process which ensures their freshness. Some snails are canned with the shells sold separately so home cooks in France and abroad can prepare their snails any way they want.

One Burgundian cookery book explains that a dish made from snails not from Burgundy should not have the words *escargots de Bourgogne* in its title. This is arguable. If it's a species, surely a Polish *escargot de Bourgogne* has every bit

as much right to recognition as a local one. The EC commissioners could have a field day with that one.

Enough theory. A mollusc which fed the Roman scientist, Pliny the Elder, and which the Gauls eccentrically ate for dessert was good enough for us. We decided to find out how three inventive New Burgundians, including Jacques Lameloise, turned a snail from a conventional appetizer on everybody's menu into a gastronomic rarity.

In a winter garden ambience of green wicker chairs, potted plants and a retro piano, Armand Poinsot was my second snail provider at Chez Camille, Arnay-le-Duc. And if snails come from abroad, so does the occasional chef: at Le Monte Cristo, Moneteau, Californian Bob Waggoner has followed in the footsteps of the midWestern food writer Patricia

Workers and snail shells chez Billot

Wells, and become a figure on the French gastronomic landscape. Though jealous chauvinistic locals have twice uprooted the signposts from Auxerre to his restaurant near the River Yonne, Bob has persevered and is now thoroughly integrated into the snail scene.

And here are the three chefs' variations on a theme. Note how these recipes should look from the photographs. The snail has come a long way since Pliny the Elder's time.

*Chez Camille,
Arnay-le-Duc*

EMBEURRÉE D'ESCARGOTS DE BOURGOGNE AUX HERBES FRAÎCHES

Snails wrapped in cabbage leaves with fresh herbs. As you won't be able to drink Jacques Lameloise's house Chardonnay, I suggest a Rully Premier Cru 'Gresigny' from H et P Jacqueson. Recipe of Jacques Lameloise. Serves 6.

8 cabbage leaves
6 dozen escargots de Bourgogne
1¾oz/50g (3⅓ tbs) butter
2 tbs finely chopped shallots
2oz/60g each carrot, bulb-fennel and onion, diced
2½oz/75g (heaped 1 cup) mushrooms, diced
3½ fl oz/100ml (scant 1 cup) white burgundy
1 tbs double (heavy) cream
fresh tarragon, chives, parsley and chervil, each finely chopped

Blanch the cabbage leaves in boiling, salted water for 5 minutes, then plunge into cold water.

Melt some of the butter and fry the snails over low heat with the shallots. In another pan, simmer the diced vegetables gently for 10 minutes in the remaining butter with the wine and cream. When the liquid is reduced by half, add all the herbs, except the chervil, then add the snails and shallots. Set aside to cool.

Flatten the cabbage leaves and fill each with 12 snails. Roll up, then wrap each 'package' in cling film (plastic wrap). Steam the 'packages' for 15 minutes.

Unwrap and place each cabbage role on individual plates. Cover with a layer of the vegetable mixture, sprinkle with the chervil and serve.

ESCARGOTS DE BOURGOGNE RÔTIS, SUR MOUSSELINE DE CHOUX-FLEURS SAUCE MOUTARDE ET PAVOT BLEU

Snails with a mousseline of cauliflower, mustard mayonnaise and blue poppy seeds. This last exotica can be replaced by ordinary poppy seeds. We ate this with an equally exotic wine: a rare red from Chablis – a 1989 Bourgogne Rouge Domaine Etienne Defaix. It was suitably earthy to accompany the snails. Recipe of Bob Waggoner. Serves 2.

3 tbs strong Dijon mustard
1 tbs red-wine vinegar
3 egg yolks
8fl oz/250ml (1 cup) groundnut (peanut) oil
16 escargots de Bourgogne
8oz/250g (2 cups) fine dried breadcrumbs
½ head of cauliflower
salt, pepper
3½fl oz/100ml (scant ½ cup) single (light) cream
butter for frying snails
1 tsp blue poppy seeds
1 tsp fresh chives cut into lengths ¼ inch/0.5cm long
FOR THE SAUCE
3 shallots, finely chopped
½ tbs butter
3½fl oz/100ml (scant ½ cup) white cooking wine
3½fl oz/100ml (scant ½ cup) dry vermouth
7fl oz/200ml (1 cup less 2 tbs) single (light) cream
1 tbs strong Dijon mustard

Make a mayonnaise with the mustard, vinegar, egg yolks and oil. Dip the snails, 1 at a time, in the mayonnaise and then roll them in the breadcrumbs and reserve.

Boil the cauliflower in salted water until you can easily squash it with a fork. Drain well, and while still hot, purée in a blender or a food processor with the cream and salt and pepper to make a mousseline. Reserve.

To make the sauce, sweat the chopped shallots in butter in a casserole, then deglaze with white wine and vermouth. Reduce until nearly dry. Add the cream and mustard and reduce again until the consistency of a thick sauce.

Gently fry the snails on both sides in a little butter. To serve, put 8 snails on each place with 2 tbs cauliflower mousseline and the mustard sauce. Sprinkle with poppy seeds and chives and serve.

RISSOLES D'ESCARGOTS AUX PÂTES FRAÎCHES AUX CHAMPIGNONS SAUVAGES

Snail rissoles with fresh pasta and wild mushrooms in a red wine sauce. We ate this with a red wine light and earthy enough to go perfectly with snails. To each his taste, and served from cut-glass decanters at Chez Camille, the 1988 Hautes-Côtes de Beaune from Gabriel Demangeot, a cousin of the Poinsots, was very much to mine. Recipe of Armand Poinsot. Serves 4.

24 escargots de Bourgogne
³⁄₄oz/20g (scant ¹⁄₃ cup) mushrooms
1 egg white, lightly beaten
flour and dried breadcrumbs for
rolling rissoles
sunflower oil for frying
salt, pepper
FOR THE BEURRE OSCAR
¹⁄₂ tbs butter
1 small clove garlic, crushed
1 shallot, finely chopped
FOR THE RED WINE SAUCE
³⁄₄ pint/500ml (2 cups) red burgundy
a few meat bones

1 bouquet garni of fresh thyme,
parsley and bay leaf
1 onion, chopped
¹⁄₂ tbs flour
salt, pepper

To make the red wine sauce, mix all the ingredients together in a saucepan, stirring the flour into the wine. Bring to the boil, then simmer for 1 hour. Strain and set aside.

To make the *beurre Oscar*, beat the butter with the other ingredients to make a paste.

Finely chop the snails and mushrooms and mix together. Melt the *beurre Oscar*, then add it to the snails with the egg white. Using a wooden spoon, shape into 24 small rissoles. Roll in flour, then lightly in breadcrumbs. Fry the rissoles lightly in sunflower oil until golden.

Re-heat the sauce. Cover each plate with the sauce, then place 6 rissoles on each plate and serve with thin, fresh noodles and wild mushrooms in season, such as *ceps*, *girolles* and *pleurottes*.

FRESHWATER FRIENDS

If people get to look like their pets, so do some resemble their food. A Frenchman seeing a *rosbif* at his roast beef may cry 'Cannibalism!'; likewise, an Englishman observing a 'Frog' stuck into a plate of *grenouilles*.

I've never understood why *grenouilles* should send such shivers down a foreign gullet; they are one of Burgundy's most tasty specialities – as served, simply, in melted butter, garlic and parsley by Georges Blanc in his new Vonnas *bistrot*, accompanied by a white Mâcon-Azé from his own vineyard. Neither fish nor fowl, perhaps, but a delicious bit of both.

Finding one's frogs is another matter. A cautionary tale recounts how a retired local politician decided to do his bit for the dying French art of batrachoculture. At his château in the Saône-et-Loire he constructed a number of ponds for breeding. He filled the first with frog spawn. The summer nights were filled with a gentle croaking. There was a second pond, however, and more spawning. And a third, and so forth, until the night was rent with a chorus of coax! coax! to fill the Hollywood Bowl, never mind a Greek theatre. The politician's wife divorced him. And, on a diet of sleeping pills and frogs, the insomniac persevered for the greater glory of French gastronomy.

As Aristotle, not Aristophanes (author of 'The Frogs') said: 'A true cook is one who enjoys being in the kitchen.' And none exudes more relish for his art than Bernard Loiseau, concocting his *grenouilles à la purée d'ail et au jus de persil*. Like many of today's crayfish, most frog's legs come from eastern Europe. The young Côte d'Or waiter who served Bernard Loiseau's admirable frog dish, was realistic: 'Patriotic? Only when it comes to French quality. A frog needs good legs like a Bluebell girl. If we can't provide the ingredients, *tant pis*. It's what's on the plate that counts.'

Very occasionally, in the remote corners of the Brionnais or the Morvan, you see an old codger at his frog pond, scooping out lunch. Most frog's legs, however, are eaten in restaurants. And at Chez Camille, Armand Poinsot serves *crème de grenouilles aux perles du Japon*. The creamy, garlicky sauce contains manioc – transparent tapioca-like pearls. 'Clients sometimes ask me for the Japanese pearls on the side,' Armand joked, 'to offer as presents to their wives.'

He believes a good meal is a show you share with loved ones. According to the category of restaurant, it's Grand Opera or Café-Théâtre. 'I'd love to open a single bistro in a Morvan village,' he said. 'Even if there was nothing around except the cars of visitors!' Plus, I hoped, his *goujonette de carpe* (carp fishcakes in a red wine sauce).

George Blanc's 'L'Ancienne Auberge' bistrot, Vonnas

The Morvan ponds and little lakes, shrouded in morning mists which the sun gently disperses, are a fly fisherman's paradise. Three hundred years ago, they were the fisheries for the Catholic monasteries' Friday diet, providing pike, tench, carp and trout. The four seasons are marked here by the most extreme climatic conditions. Even at its bleakest, it is a land of ferns and fir trees burgeoning with natural vigour; from bog to bracken-covered hillside, health-giving herbs abound – anis-flavoured chervil, *citronella* (lemon grass), wild celery. Previously, it was the women of the Morvan, known for their

Above: Morvan fishing lake near Saulieu

Left: 'Big Six' chef Georges Blanc and his son Frédérique

Left: Verdun-Sur-Le Doubs, home of the fish stew Pauchouse

good milk, who went to Paris to suckle the babies of the rich, leaving their husbands in charge of the children.

Luckily, those good old days are no more. But it has left a void, not yet filled by tourism. The Morvan is poor, its lakes provide the drink of richer places, and its granite, acid soil is inhospitable to the cattle farming to which farmers stubbornly hold. 'We must change the thinking', says Thierry de Montalembert, whose family own the Château de la Roche and 1350 acres of forest, ponds and lakes.

He and his brother, Gilles, have restocked their fish ponds as a commercial venture. The French, Thierry told us, are not carp eaters, but restaurateurs like Poinsot are educating them. And fishermen can rent fishing daily – and keep the carp, tench, *gardons* (a freshwater fish) and pike they catch.

Thierry and Gilles also produce quality smoked or marinated trout and carp fillets. 'With carp, I'd drink an Aligoté,' Thierry recommended. 'It's sharp and strong, helps the taste of the fish. Whereas smoked trout is more subtle, requiring a fruity, flowery Chablis.'

This reminded me of the unusual *quenelles de brochet à la chablisienne,*

made by Alain Mahieu at the Hotel de l'Étoile, Chablis. It was a pike dish that defies adequate translation; a quenelle is not a sausage, though it looks like one. Mahieu's sauce was a variation on the better known *sauce nantua*, not strictly Burgundian, though made with Chablis. Sensibly, the bar serves vintage wines of the region by the glass.

In a Chablis backstreet, there is a gate you would hardly notice. The names René et Vincent Dauvissat are carved on a tiny barrel. Beyond the gate is a courtyard with modest brick house and a rough

Charolais cattle near Verdun-Sur-le-Doubs

Château du Nozet, Pouilly-sur-Loire

workshop full of wine cartons and hosepipes and viticultural tools, where a woman is having trouble with a bottling machine. She reveals herself as Françoise, wife of Vincent, and, yes, her husband will receive me in a moment. For this is where perhaps *the* Chablis is made (three Premier Crus, two Grands Crus). The Dauvissats don't even have a price list, let alone publicity. Every bottle is sold privately.

Vincent gave me a memorable tasting in his musty, cobwebby cellar. His *pipette*, a plunging siphon, went into a barrel of 1990 'Sechet', and filled my glass. What attack! What a finish! Rich, concentrated, staying long with me . . .

I was quite unable to spit it. And what, I asked, would Vincent eat with such a wine? I expected some great and elaborate dish. 'Well, I'd give it a few years,' he said. 'And then it will be really good with *quenelles à la chablisienne*. Cooked in 'Sechet', too? A doubtful smile: 'Well, maybe.'

Another wine mated with fish is Pouilly Fumé (not to be confused with Pouilly-Fuissé, also made in Burgundy but 100 miles away). The Nièvre's one claim to viticultural fame is the wine made at Pouilly-sur-Loire, mainly with the Sauvignon grape typical of that river's white wines.

Baron Patrick de Ladoucette, descendant of a Victorian banking family, at his fake Renaissance Château du Nozet has a very genuine modern *chai*, with vinification techniques as demanding as those in Champagne. The climate and silex soil on the slopes overlooking the Loire valley are, ostensibly, ideal for Sauvignon but it takes a Ladoucette to get it right.

Why, *Fumé* – 'smoked'? Several theories: the noble wine was said to produce a smoky aroma; the silex in the chalky soil gives a mineral taste, like gunpowder. Anyway, it goes well with smoked

A top Pouilly Fumé made at Château du Nozet

salmon, shellfish and grilled river fish which are more or less the same in the Loire as the Saône.

We found the Coq Hardi filled with English gentlefolk, enjoying their glasses of the pale, greenish wine while ordering from Jean-Claude Astruc's value-for-money menu. The Brits, good at sniffing out a gastronomic bargain, head for the Michelin Red R restaurants like bears to a honeypot. There was a choice of pike mousse, *sandre* (a delicate river fish) with sorrel, and fried roach (little fish like whitebait), accompanied by a wild sunset across the Loire, a scent of lime blossom, and an '88 Prestiges des Fines Caillottes from Jean Babiot at Les Loges.

The most popular Burgundian fish dish calls for no grand wine. And, for *pauchouse* at its popular best, go to the Hotel des Trois Maures at Verdun-sur-le-Doubs. A silly comparison is made with bouillabaisse; whereas that Marseilles dish is now absurdly expensive, its much more basic freshwater cousin is the food of riverside *Relais Routiers*. This fisherman's stew contains anything that's been fished fresh – pike, carp, small tench or perch, and is made with Aligoté and cream. When I asked what I should drink with my *pauchouse*, the waitress just said: 'White wine.' This was not the hotel Côte d'Or – and none the worse for that, either.

New Burgundians have started mixing fish and meat in the same dish – and most successfully. 'That's the way it's evolved, since *nouvelle cuisine* had its day,' said Jean-Pierre Silva, serving us pike with a pig's trotter and lentils. Curiously, in that very same small village of Bouilland, at La Bonne Auberge, a restaurant of no pretensions other than to provide a good meal for under the equivalent of £10 ($18), I had one of my favourite Burgundian experiences – a chicken and eel fricassée. We shall hear more of Bernard Denis, I hope.

LA FRICASSÉE DE POULET À L'ANGUILLE

An interesting mix of chicken and eel in cream and wine. We drank a 1990 Bourgogne Aligoté from Bernard Jacob at Savigny-lés-Beaune. Beware: even in a modest restaurant, a bottle of Bourgogne Aligoté can cost the same as the meal. Recipe of Bernard Denis. Serves 4.

1 eel, weighing 2¼ lb/1kg, cut into
steaks 1 inch/2.5cm thick
butter and vegetable oil for sautéing
2 onions, finely chopped
2 carrots, finely chopped
1 leek, white part only, finely
chopped
3 tbs flour
1 tbs mild paprika
1 chicken, weighing 2¾ lb/1.2kg, cut
into 8-10 pieces
1¼ pints/750ml (3 cups) Aligoté
burgundy
salt, pepper
7oz/200g (3 cups) button mushrooms
¾ pint/500ml (2 cups) double
(heavy) cream
30g/1oz (2 tbs) butter

1 tbs flour
juice of 1 lemon
1 tsp chopped, fresh, dill

Soak the eel cutlets in cold water for 30 minutes.

Meanwhile, heat the butter and oil in a flameproof casserole and sauté the vegetables. Combine the flour and paprika and use it to dust the chicken pieces. Sauté the chicken in a frying pan until golden brown on all sides, then add to the casserole with the vegetables. Cook for 10 minutes over a medium heat.

Strain the eel and add to the casserole. Pour in the wine and enough water to cover, then season and simmer until tender, about 20 minutes.

Meanwhile, sauté the mushrooms for 2 minutes in a little oil.

Transfer the chicken and eel to a serving dish and keep warm. Strain the sauce, then pour in the cream and reduce by half.

Make a *beurre manié* with the flour and butter and use to thicken the sauce. Adjust the seasoning. Add the lemon juice and mushrooms to the sauce, then spoon over the chicken and eel and sprinkle with dill. Serve at once.

Mijoté de Lentilles au Pied de Cochon, Dos de Brochet rôti au Vinaigre d'Herbes

A stew of lentils and pigs' trotters with pike roasted with herb vinegar. This extraordinary-sounding dish was quite wonderful, especially served with a treat of a wine from Jean-Pierre Silva's own cellar: a 1970 Echézeaux Grand Cru from Morin Père et Fils, smooth, velvety, opening with the meal – a perfect balance for the meat and fish. Don't believe red doesn't go with fish! It's a matter of taste and wine. Recipe of Jean-Pierre Silva. Serves 4.

8oz/250g (heaped 1 cup) green lentils
2 pigs' trotters, cooked and tender enough for the meat to fall off the bones
3½oz/100g (7 tbs) butter
½ onion, chopped
bouquet garni of fresh thyme, parsley and bay leaf
¾ pint/500ml (2 cups) red burgundy
8fl oz/250ml (1 cup) veal stock
salt, pepper
2oz/60g (¼ cup) lard
4 pike fillets, about 5oz/150g each
4 tbs herb vinegar

Soak the lentils for 2 hours.

Cut the trotter meat into small cubes. Melt 2oz/60g (½ stick) butter in a flameproof casserole and fry the onion until golden. Add the trotters, lentils, bouquet garni and wine. Bring to the boil, then stir in the veal stock and salt and pepper. Cover and cook in a medium to low oven for about 45 minutes; the lentils must not turn to a purée.

In a frying pan, melt the remaining butter and lard (the fat gives a more rustic taste) and fry the pike fillets for about 1 minute on each side. Pour off the fat, then deglaze the pan with the herb vinegar and reduce by half.

Place the lentils on 4 plates, then top with the fish fillets and spoon a little of the pan juices over each portion.

QUENELLES DE BROCHET À LA CHABLISIENNE

Quenelles of pike in a thick, rich Chablis sauce. At the moderately priced Hotel de l'Étoile, you can enjoy a glass of a really great vintage Chablis with this dish. It deserves it. Recipe of Alain Mahieu. Serves 4.

¾ pint/500ml (2 cups) milk
3½oz/100g (7 tbs) butter
7oz/200g (1¾ cups) flour
8 eggs
2¼lb/1kg pike fillets, any bones and skin removed and flaked
¾ pint/500ml (2 cups) fish stock
salt, pepper
few knobs of butter
1 tbs plain flour
3½oz/100g (⅔ cup) shallots, finely chopped
freshly grated nutmeg
¾ pint/500ml (2 cups) Chablis
extra butter

Make a *panade*, a thick mixture to bind the quenelles. Boil the milk and add the butter. Off the heat, add the liquid to the flour and stir well. Return to heat and cook until nearly dry, stirring often.

Beat in 4 eggs, 1 at a time, then stir in the pike and remaining eggs. Pass the mixture through a nylon sieve (strainer) twice. Leave to cool. Season to taste.

With a wooden spoon, shape the mixture into 8 quenelles. Poach them in the fish stock.

For the sauce, make a roux with the butter and flour. Stir in some of the fish stock until smooth. In another pan, combine the shallots, nutmeg and wine and season with pepper. Reduce by half and add to the sauce. Adjust the seasoning and finish off with a few extra knobs of butter, beating constantly. Pass through a fine-meshed, conical sieve.

Drain the quenelles well, then put 3 on each serving plate. Spoon over the sauce and serve at once.

LES GRENOUILLES À LA PURÉE D'AIL ET AU JUS DE PERSIL

Frogs' legs with a garlic purée and parsley sauce. This is how a top New Burgundian makes frogs' legs into a gastronomic delicacy. Don't be put off by the amount of garlic: Bernard has a subtle process for making it palatable. It is best eaten with a good, full-bodied white, like Loiseau's 1988 Chablis Premier Cru from Domaine Laroche. Recipe of Bernard Loiseau. Serves 4.

3¹⁄₂ oz/100g fresh parsley
salt, freshly milled pepper
1 head of garlic
4fl oz/125ml (¹⁄₂ cup) milk
4 dozen frogs' legs
2 tbs olive oil
knob of butter

Wash the parsley and remove the stems. Cook the leaves in boiling, salted water for 3–4 minutes, then drain and plunge into cold water. Purée in a blender or food processor. Reserve.

Break the garlic into separate cloves and, without peeling, plunge the cloves into boiling water for 2 minutes. They will now peel easily. Change the water and bring to the boil. Boil the cloves for 7–8 minutes, then drain and repeat the process 5 or 6 times until the garlic is well cooked. This takes away the 'kick' of the garlic without losing the taste. Slice each clove in half and remove the green germ from each, then purée the cloves. Mix with the milk and season. Reserve.

Salt and pepper the frogs' legs and fry them in very hot olive oil with a knob of butter for 2–3 minutes, until golden brown. Pat dry with kitchen paper (paper towels).

Meanwhile, combine the parsley purée and ¹⁄₂ tbs water in a saucepan to make a sauce. Heat and season.

Spoon the parsley sauce over 4 plates and put the garlic purée in the centre of each. Arrange the frogs' legs on each plate. Serve at once.

PAUCHOUSE

The classic river fish dish, as made by *la patronne* and her son at the Hotel des Trois Maures, Verdun-sur-le-Doubs. The Doubs is a tributary of the Saône and, according to local fishermen, the fish is fresher. This would be eaten with a simple Aligoté burgundy. Recipe of Madame Vithu. Serves 4.

3½ pints/2 litres (9 cups) white
wine, preferably Aligoté
2 tsp marc de Bourgogne *or Cognac*
10oz/300g garlic, crushed, plus 1
extra clove
1 sprig fresh thyme
2¼ lb/1kg pike, heads reserved
2¼ lb/1kg tench, heads reserved
2¼ lb/1kg perch, heads reserved
1 tbs flour
½ oz/15g (1 tbs) butter
salt, pepper
8 slices French bread

In a saucepan, flame the wine by lighting the marc in a heated ladle and pouring it over the heated wine. When the flames die down, add the garlic, thyme and fish heads and simmer for 1 hour to make the fish stock.

Strain the stock and use it to poach the fish for about 20 minutes, or until cooked through. Keep the fish warm.

Make a roux with the flour and butter, then stir in the poaching liquid to make a smooth sauce. Season.

Meanwhile, toast the bread and rub with the extra garlic.

Arrange the fish on a serving platter, then spoon over the sauce. Arrange the garlic toast around the dish and serve at once.

THE FAMOUS COCK

A chicken is as good as its sauce.

OLD BURGUNDIAN SAYING

Nobody knows where *coq au vin* originated; surely made with Chambertin, the most illustrious of local reds, it must have been enjoyed by the Dukes of Burgundy. Rather sensibly, they would eat it in the vast kitchens of the Palais des Ducs, Dijon, where the aromas of the cooking would linger rather than evaporate in the wastes of a chilly banqueting hall.

At a fine nineteenth-century manor house, once surrounded by vineyards but now emeshed in a sprawling Dijon suburb, we were entertained by Jean-Philippe Lecat, a former Minister of Culture, and his mother, Madeleine. Passionate about all things Burgundian, he was an oracle on the evolution of the cuisine.

'In the fifteenth century, there were two cuisines,' he explained. 'The Dukes ate meat, especially game – roasts with spices from Constantinople. The serfs made do with cheese and vegetables – especially onions and garlic, like the Provençals.'

The culinary class barriers began to fall in the nineteenth century. Parisians, like Proust, spent more time at their Burgundy châteaux. They hired peasant cooks. The lady of the house taught them *cuisine bourgeoise*, and, in turn, they brought local recipes and superb produce to the *châtelaine*, resulting in a healthy cross fertilization of gastronomy. This is why the origins are hard to define.

'But we know that chicken began to lose its luxury status in the Thirties,' Monsieur Lecat told us. 'The Right led a campaign against the Popular Front with the slogan: "The workers want to eat chicken!"' And now they do. And very good chicken at that.

Coq au vin appears in the country cookery book of La Famille Vincenot. Or it can be done more elaborately. Jean-Pierre Silva does the cock's thighs with tiny cubes of Swiss chard, simmered in wine for 5 hours. The breast is poached for a mere minute, and the dish is served with 'spaghetti' of thin vegetables – carrots, turnips and Swiss chard. Only the

Summerhouse at Jean-Philippe Lecat's home, Dijon

Restaurateur Jean-Pierre Silva of the Vieux Moulin, Bouilland

best poultry will do, of course. And the best of the best comes from the flat Bresse region of southern Burgundy with its *appellation d'origine contrôlée*. Each bird must wear its badge of provenance, like the better wines and certain cheeses.

At the Bresse farm of Didier Grand-jean, near Louhans, every morning 3500 birds come flying out of the sheds which protect them from night-prowling rats and foxes. On the dot of 8.30, they breakfast on cornflour and buttermilk; then, full of the joys of their patriotic colours – red crests, white feathers, blue feet –

86

cocks and hens together flap wings, fight a bit, and free-range all day over land with 10 square metres grazing for each bird, as required by the appellation.

Nearby was the Ferme Auberge du Grand Colombier, a half-timbered Bressane farmhouse with overhanging eaves and strangely arabic chimneys. In the wood-fired bread oven, the family's own chickens are cooked for the Sunday hordes. 'With a little less cream for anyone on a diet,' said Madame de Bourg, the farmer's wife, obligingly.

Small poultry-raisers with hampers of pigeons, ducks, chickens, capons, turkeys and geese flock to the famous Monday market at Louhans. The noise is deafening, the bargaining tough. 'I never buy Bresse at market,' said poultry dealer Madame Mieral from Montrevel-en-Bresse. 'I can't be sure it's been raised to the standards required by law. We buy direct from the big farmers.' So what was she doing here, I wondered? A queue of hopeful sellers were lining up with pigeons. Madame Mieral felt their breasts and, if satisfied, popped them into her cages and paid with cash. 'Pigeons have no feeding rules,' she said. 'As long as they get plenty of snails and grass, they're fine!'

Free-range Bresse chickens taking their morning exercise

Ferme Auberge du Grand Colombier, typical Bresse farm-inn near Marboz

Right: Herb stall at Chalon-sur-Saône market

Madame Mieral's most illustrious client is Georges Blanc, whose devotion to Bresse poultry is unconditional. His Vonnas restaurant-and-shopping complex is like a Hollywood version of a southern Burgundian village. It should be renamed Blancville-en-Bresse. For everything on the 'lot' is Georges Blanc: warehouse converted into hotel with helipad; flower-decked canal; village shop selling Georges Blanc ceramics and 270 French wines, including GB's own; L'Ancien Auberge bistrot where GB's son, Fréderique, is chef. (The prices one-quarter of the GB restaurant in the hotel.)

One difference from a film set: the star is always visible, in his chef's whites, everywhere at once, keeping an eye on all operations – from the bread in the GB bakery, to the paintings in the GB art gallery. Georges Blanc is entrepreneur, artist and writer. With his sharp eye, he quietly helped Carey set up her photo of his famous *fricassée de poulet de Bresse a la Crème*. This exquisite Bresse pullet, painstakingly fattened, is served with *crêpes vonnassiennes* (potato pancakes). It had a nostalgic chicken taste I'd almost forgotten, even if Bresse poultry, raised as it is in such natural conditions, tends to be a little more muscular than what I am used to.

Georges Blanc does not yet make red wine at his own Domaine d'Azenay winery (the American word used appropriately by his ultra-modern female *caviste*, Colette Morel), but would drink nothing else with chicken. His preference was a Volnay, from the Côte de Beaune with a fine, delicate bouquet to match light, white meat.

And the Volnay I would choose, partly because she is such a remarkable character, would be that of Armande Monthelie-Duhairet known to the wine world as 'Mademoiselle'. 'Spinster' is too staid a word for this racy 85-year-old wine-maker with 27 acres of Volnay, Pommard and Meursault-Santenots, not to mention the lesser-known, fragrant reds of Monthelie, where her family have lived

for 300 years. Mademoiselle is alleged to have broken her hip rushing to change TV channels from a rock programme to a porno, and shocks some people with her sharp humour. *'C'est une soirée d'Écosse!'* she greets us with a raunchy cackle, using the Burgundian expression for bad weather – a Scotch afternoon – to tease her winebroker friend, Russell Hone, a Scot who was showing us round the vineyards.

Russell was sent down to the cellar to fetch a really good wine for what Mademoiselle calls *'mon p'tit apéritif'*. She was delighted with his choice of strong, golden '86 Meursault-Santenots (first name is the commune or village; the second name is the parcel of the vineyard); despite Georges Blanc's insistence on red with chicken, this white would not exactly be an insult to a *poulet Gaston Gérard*, Mademoiselle's favourite chicken dish.

Poultry market, Louhans, in the Bresse region

Armande Monthelie-Duhairet (known as 'Mademoiselle'), Côte de Beaune winemaker

Capons are also a Burgundian favourite. These neutered cockerels, as raised by antique dealer-chicken farmer Jean-Pierre Quignard and his son Emmanuel, supply the Hostellerie du Vieux Moulin. Jean-Pierre Silva recommends: 'Slip a sliced truffle under the skin and roast slowly on a spit.' It sounded too simple for him, I said. He laughed and continued: 'That's my own personal favourite – with potatoes sautéd in pig fat. There's enough for ten friends on a capon. With a few bottles of nice, light Santenay . . .' He looked ecstatic at the mere thought.

There were other comparatively simple poultry dishes to be enjoyed during our stay. At a *table d'hôte* stopover at Arnay-le-Duc, Simone and Armand Picard gave us turkey escalopes for dinner round the family table – superb value for money at the equivalent of about £7/$16: kir, soup, salad, turkey, cheese and chocolate cake with plenty of red Passe-Tout-Grains. 'Hard to get now,' commented our attentive host. 'Burgundians don't think it's worth the trouble of making everyday wines.' It was light, a bit acid but refreshing on a hot evening.

Also memorable were recipes of Marc Millot of the Lion d'Or, Saulieu, and Jean-Claude Astruc at Le Coq Hardi, Pouilly-sur-Loire. The workers' chicken has come a long way since the Thirties.

Early morning at Ratte near Louhans

Fine Côte de Beaune wines in Armande Monthelie-Duhairet's cellar

JAMBONETTE DE VOLAILLE AU POUILLY

Stuffed chicken thighs in local wine. Monsieur Astruc recommends serving this with a Pouilly-Fumé from a small wine maker, such as Jean Babiot at Les Loges or Michel Redde's 1986 Cuvee Majorum. Recipe of Jean-Claude Astruc. Serves 6.

FOR THE STUFFING
3½ oz / 100g skinned boneless chicken breast, minced
3½ oz / 100g breast of pork, minced
3½ fl oz / 100ml marc de Bourgogne or Cognac
5 fl oz / 150ml Pouilly-Fumé, or Loire Sauvignon
1 egg
salt, pepper
1 sprig fresh parsley, chopped
3 cloves garlic, crushed

FOR THE SAUCE
¾ pint / 500ml (2 cups) chicken stock
8 fl oz / 250ml (1 cup) Pouilly-Fumé
2 egg yolks
7 fl oz / 200ml double (heavy) cream

Make the stuffing by mixing all the ingredients together, except the wine.

Stuff the boned thighs to give them back their shapes. Braise for 20 minutes in a 400°F/200°C/Gas Mark 6 with the wine.

Meanwhile, make the sauce. Reduce the stock and the wine by two-thirds. Thicken with the egg yolks and cream.

Place the thighs on a serving dish and pour over the sauce. Serve with sautéd *girolles* or other mushrooms and potatoes of your choice.

Suprême de Volaille Fermier au Jus de Vin Echalotte

Slices of free-range chicken breasts in a wine and shallot sauce, surrounded by a *galette* of crispy, thinly sliced potatoes. Marc Millot recommended a 1984 Morey-St-Denis, a remarkably good wine in a bad year, from the Société d'Exploitation de Clos de Tart (a Grand Cru vineyard).

2 large free-range chicken breasts
2 big potatoes, peeled and sliced
paper thin
8oz/250g butter
salt, pepper
For the Sauce
6 shallots, chopped
7oz/200g (1½ sticks) butter
2fl oz/60ml (5 tbs) red burgundy
2 tbs chicken stock
salt, pepper

First make the sauce. Brown the shallots in 2oz/60g (½ stick) butter, then deglaze the pan with the wine. Reduce a little and stir in the chicken stock and reduce again by half. Beat in small knobs of the remaining butter to thicken the sauce, then season with salt and pepper. Strain through a fine sieve. Reserve.

Fry the chicken in a little butter, without letting it dry out, and keep it hot in the pan.

To make the potato *galette*, heat a non-stick pan with 5oz/150g (1¼ sticks) butter. Place the potato slices in a fan shape in the pan so they overlap: they will stick together as they brown, which is correct. Add salt and pepper. When one side is browned, turn the *galette* over and brown the other side. It should be good and crispy.

Slice the chicken breasts. Place on a hot serving platter and cover with the sauce. Put the *galette* on top. (Marc Millot puts a cooked chicken bone sticking up through the *galette* on one side of the dish, so it looks like a peacock with the 'fan' of its potatoes representing the feathers.)

FRICASSÉE DE POULET DE BRESSE A LA CRÈME

Bresse chicken in cream and white burgundy, served with potato pancakes (recipe following). A traditional masterpiece from one of the Big Six maestros of Burgundy. Eat with a Volnay, or one of Mademoiselle's premier Cru Monthelie-Duresses or Monthelie-Le Meix Bataille, not as grand but as fragrant and light as Volnay. Recipe of Georges Blanc. Serves 4.

*1 large Bresse chicken, weighing
about 4lb/1.8kg
3½oz/100g butter
salt, pepper
1 onion, quartered
10 mushrooms, quartered
2 unpeeled garlic cloves, crushed
bouquet garni of fresh thyme, parsley
and bay leaf
7fl oz/200ml (scant 1 cup) dry white
burgundy
1¾ pints/1 litre (4½ cups) double
(heavy) cream*

Cut the chicken into pieces: first the legs, which are separated into thighs and drumsticks, then the wings; cut off the wing tips. Split the carcase lengthways to obtain the 2 breast fillets.

Melt the butter in a large flameproof casserole or frying pan (skillet) over high heat and add the chicken pieces. Season with salt and pepper, then add the onion, mushrooms, garlic and bouquet garni. Fry until the chicken is well browned, about 6 minutes on each side.

Deglaze with the wine and reduce. Stir in the cream and continue cooking for 25-30 minutes, until the chicken is cooked through.

Remove the chicken pieces and keep hot, then pass the sauce through a fine sieve. Emulsify in a blender or food processor. Adjust the seasoning.

Put the chicken pieces in a deep serving dish and pour over the sauce. Serve immediately with *crêpes vonnassiennes* or boiled rice.

POULET GASTON GÉRARD

Chicken pieces or legs, cooked in a wine, mustard and cheese sauce. This is a classic recipe named after the former mayor of Dijon who invented it, and launched the city's international gastronomic fair. This is a simple version by Mademoiselle, to be eaten with her 1982 Volnay 'En Champans'. Recipe of Armande Monthelie-Duhairet. Serves 4.

1 free-range chicken, weighing about
3½lb/1.5kg, cut into 8 pieces,
or 8 thighs
2oz/60g (½ stick) butter
2oz/60g (¼ cup) vegetable oil
2 wine glasses white burgundy
1 tbs cornflour (cornstarch)
4 tbs double (heavy) cream
2 tbs Dijon mustard
5oz/150g Gruyere cheese, grated
salt, pepper

Brown the chicken pieces in the butter and oil in a flameproof casserole. Put in a 350°F/180°C/Gas Mark 5 oven for 30 minutes, until cooked through.

Remove the chicken pieces from the casserole and keep warm. Deglaze the pan with the wine. Stir in the cornflour, cream, mustard and cheese, then season. Pour over the chicken pieces and brown under a pre-heated grill (broiler). Serve at once.

COQ AU VIN

The traditional cock stew in red wine sauce. Recipes are legion for this dish, as are the arguments: old bird or young? Cockerel or hen? This is a classic version, to be eaten with the same wine you use in the cooking, whether a good simple red burgundy, a St-Aubin or a Chambertin. Our recipe. Serves 4.

7oz/200g streaky bacon, cubed
24 small onions, peeled
1 tbs olive oil
1 free-range chicken, weighing about
4½ lb/2kg, cut into pieces
(see Fricassée de Poulet de Bresse a la
Crème, page 94)
salt, pepper
2 tbs flour
½ wine glass marc de Bourgogne *or*
Cognac
bouquet garni of fresh thyme, parsley
and bay leaf
1 bottle red burgundy
8 slices French bread
1 clove garlic, peeled
8oz/250g (3½ cups) button
mushrooms

In a large flameproof casserole, fry the bacon and glaze the onions in the olive oil. Remove from the pan and reserve.

Fry the chicken pieces and season, then sprinkle with the flour. When golden, flame with the marc.

Return the bacon and onions with the bouquet garni. Pour over the wine, then bring to the boil. Lower the heat and simmer, covered, for about 2½ hours, until the meat is tender.

Remove the chicken pieces, bacon and onions and reserve. Cook the sauce over a medium heat for about 30 minutes to reduce by half.

Meanwhile, toast the bread and rub with the garlic; keep warm. Sauté the mushrooms. Return the capon pieces, bacon and onions to the casserole, add the mushrooms and heat through. Serve at once with the garlic toast.

CRÊPES VONNASSIENNES

Tiny potato pancakes which go deliciously with almost any main course in the book. Also known as *crêpes de la mère Blanc*, these are an invention of Georges Blanc's mother. Makes 6.

14oz/400g (3½ sticks) butter, plus
extra for frying
1lb/500g potatoes, peeled
salt
¾ pint/500ml milk
3 tbs flour
3 eggs
4 egg whites

Begin by making clarified butter for frying: melt the butter and boil in a flameproof casserole, skimming until it is perfectly clear. Pour through a muslin (cheesecloth) sieve. Reserve.

Boil the potatoes in salt water, then purée, beating in the milk. Leave to cool.

Put the potatoes in a large bowl. Mix in the flour, the whole eggs, one at a time, then the egg whites (not beaten). Beat it progressively, without working too much, until the potatoes are the consistency of a thick custard.

In a large frying pan (skillet), heat enough butter to make an omelette. Add ¾ tbs of the potato mixture, making 6 or 7 pancakes at once: the little rounds form themselves, like fritters. Brown on one side, then turn over, and cook on the other side.

BIG BEEF

Appetite comes with eating.

RABELAIS

All roads lead to St-Christophe-en-Brionnais. From 2.30 every Thursday morning, this small, nondescript southern Burgundy town of 850 inhabitants swells to 2000 as the cattle trucks converge for the biggest of Charolais markets. It is known as *la marée blanche* (the white tide) because of the whiteness of the cattle we'd already seen dotted about the green fields like children's toys. Now they looked considerably larger.

We blinked in the chilly dawn. It was 6.30. Cattle moved and stamped everywhere. Cowmen with sticks who had arrived four hours earlier to herd their beasts into the best stalls were in need of a warming *pot-au-feu* and a *coup de rouge* (it was lunchtime for them), and the clatter and chatter at the Café du Champ de Foire soon woke us up.

Jacques Despierres, wholesaler from Roanne, arrived in a Mercedes Turbo with his pretty wife, Christine, who does the accounts – yuppies among the yokels. Prompt at 8.30 when the buying began,

Jacques was perilously close to a heifer's hindquarters for a man so neatly dressed.

'With Charolais, you look for plump behinds,' he said. 'The muscles make them good to eat.' He made a deal, and cut his number on the rump with scissors. The heifers he bought that morning would be transported later to the slaughterhouse in Roanne, just south of the Burgundy border, and their meat delivered to butchers the next day.

These were *Label Rouge Charolais*, guaranteed free from hormone-injection, fattened on the rich, mineral-impregnated grass of the fields around Oyé, not more than twenty miles away – the best grazing in France outside Normandy. 'It's like with wine,' Jacques explained. 'When you know where the grapes are grown, you've more confidence in the quality.' Each beast wears its *Label Rouge appellation* on its ear. There were huge, thin bulls for export, potent breeding bulls, baby bulls, bulls with rings in their noses. And a mighty mooing from the calves.

'That's where the trouble begins,' Jacques continued. 'Breeders find it more profitable to sell three-year-old calves to the Italians for them to fatten back home.' While cattle leave France too young, cheap meat is imported from Ireland and Germany, and the French meat industry, increasingly non-competitive, suffers.' According to a Burgundian butcher friend in Provence: 'I give it two years. Either quality French meat will catch on as a luxury, once-a-week treat – or I'll shut up shop! These days, even the supermarkets are going for better quality.'

The problems of Charolais beef faded away as our knives cut into a juicy *côte de boeuf*, barbecued on a braise of vine stocks and our sharpened noses sniffed an '87 *Nuits-St-Georges* Premier Cru Clos des Foréts St-Georges. 'Simple grilled meat puts the sturdier reds into perspective,' said our host, Jean-Pierre de Smet. 'My own taste is for lighter, elegant wines of finesse.' It was certainly lighter than

Farm barn at St-Thibaut in the Côte d'Or

Right: Domaine d'Arlot, wine property near Nuits St-Georges

my idea of a Nuits St-Georges, but pleasantly so. 'I hardly ever chaptalize – add sugar – to increase the alcoholic content. That's not my style.'

Jean-Pierre, a dashing former ocean yachtsman from Nice, and his Parisian wife, Lise, entertain informally at Domaine d'Arlot, their noble eighteenth-century château, and the nearest thing we'd seen to a Burgundian wine-maker's grand home. Bordeaux producers have the monopoly on châteaux, while here even the wealthiest tend to live in comparatively modest village houses. It comes from a tradition of frugality and charitable works: the original vineyards were owned by monasteries.

With its enchanted garden, topiary maze and vineyards surrounding the house, Domaine d'Arlot is far from grandiose. Newcomers to the wine game, the de Smets' first harvest was in 1987, and they were still three weeks away from their fifth. Then the dining-room would be stripped bare, except for the fine ceramic stove, to feed thirty harvesters every day for ten days, plus the odd British wine shipper or restaurateur dropping in for a vintage freebie. Lise did not seem daunted. 'I try to give them some-

Châteauneuf, 12th-century fortified village in the Côte d'Or

thing different every day of their stay,' she said. '*Boeuf daube* (braised beef stew) or *blanquette de veau* (veal in cream sauce).'

With this veal classic in a white sauce, Mâcon *vigneron* Jean-Luc Terrier favoured a young white wine like his dry, fruity Mâcon-Villages, preferring his oaky, fuller-bodied St-Véran with roast veal. Vincent Dauvissat would drink his exceptional Chablis with a roast, too, even a vintage one. Rules, it seemed, were made to be broken or re-written according to personal taste. Colette Morel would willingly drink her white Mâcon-Azé with a

steak. 'Red Mâcon is only for game and cheese,' she said firmly.

Burgundian recipes for pork, lamb and veal, however good the meat, are not as interesting as elsewhere in France. Yet, the great chefs of yesterday made their names with beef – like Alexandre Dumaine's world-famous *boeuf braisé* in the old days of the Hotel Côte d'Or, Saulieu. Notable exceptions exist, of course. And what better example than 36-year-old Christophe Cussac's *tête de veau aux simples du potager*, a calf's head with aromatic garnishing from the herb garden (chives,

Vineyard near Beaune, late autumn

celery, thyme, tarragon, bay leaf, celery, chervil), plus a touch of ginger.

This earthy miracle, far too ambitious for an amateur cook, is worth the detour to L'Abbaye St-Michel, Tonnerre. This is a somewhat staid Relais et Châteaux hotel, where Christophe's father, former engineer Daniel Cussac, has engineered a tenth-century Benedictine abbey into late twentieth-century designer medieval – refectory turned into low-lit, vaulted, tapestry-hung dining-room with Muzak playing (the bane of posh nosheries everywhere: who needs Swan Lake with a Bresse chicken?). The best things about L'Abbaye St-Michel, however, are its romantic country setting, with views of Notre-Dame tower and the Épineuil vineyards; the high-tech kitchens, brainchild of Cussac *père's* time-and-motion study to avoid clashes of temperament and crashes of waiters; and the *haute cuisine* of Cussac *fils*, one of a group of adventurous young French chefs who try their latest recipes out on each other. 'There's no jealousy, no secrets,' Christophe said. 'Just friendly rivalry.'

Surely, sometimes, they must want to cut each others' throats, mustn't they? Chefs, theatrical as they nowadays are, don't bitch each other in front of strangers.

And no exception was another theatrical New Burgundian, Jean-Paul Thibert, one of Dijon's best. Overlooking a sunny courtyard near a rippling fountain and bandstand, his restaurant also looks beyond Burgundy for its inspiration. Maryse Thibert, his wife, told us: 'It's boring just to be stuck with regional cooking. All over France, after an excess of 'fat' and an overdose of 'thin' cooking, now we're reaching a correct balance.' Jean-Paul's richly rolling R's bore witness to his Bresse origins. 'You either love or hate what I

Agricultural awards for Charolais cattle

make,' he said. 'People don't come back here for the same thing because I'm always developing new ideas.'

His treatment of beef, however, was comparatively simple for a New Burgundian – Charolais rumpsteak and morel mushrooms. And all the better for it, too. Best not to fuss about with a steak just the right texture, and with those essential grains of fat giving it a speckled effect. 'I'm never original for originality's sake,' Jean-Paul continued. 'There's this myth that Burgundian cooking is necessarily heavy. We have to educate foreigners. Americans like my lighter dishes, but that doesn't stop them enjoying a traditional *boeuf bourguignon*, too. It's a question of balance.'

Jean-Pierre Silva makes his not so traditionally: with a calf's foot and oxtail in the sauce, then a fillet of beef added at the end of cooking – rare, medium and well-done. Straighter versions came from Christiane Gutigny at a memorable family Sunday lunch, and from Simone Picard at Arnay-le-Duc.

Good to serve with any beef dish would be Madeleine Lecat's *pommes de terre à la Mère Chichenaque*. So let's start with those.

*The Saône
river at
Chauvort*

POMMES DE TERRE À LA MÈRE CHICHENAQUE

The smallest fried potatoes served in a cream, vinegar and parsley sauce. Recipe of Madeleine Lecat. Serves 6.

2oz/60g (½ stick) butter
4 tbs olive or sunflower oil
salt, pepper
2¼ lb/1kg tiny new potatoes, peeled
1 tbs wine vinegar
¾ pint/500ml (2 cups) double (heavy) cream
6 sprigs fresh parsley, finely chopped

Heat the butter and oil in a large frying pan (skillet). Season and fry the potatoes until crispy brown. Remove from the pan and pat dry with absorbent kitchen paper (paper towels). Keep hot.

Pour off any excess fat, then deglaze the pan with the vinegar. Stir in the cream and parsley and heat through, then pour over the potatoes. Serve at once.

BOEUF BOURGUIGNON

The region's classic beef-and-wine stew, as served at the Picards' *table d'hôte*. I suggest serving it with a 1987 Savigny-les-Beaune from Girard-Vollot. It is fragrant and quite weighty enough for the stew. Recipe of Simone Picard. Serves 4.

3⅓ lb/1.5kg braising beef, cut into chunks
60g/2oz (½ stick) butter
2 tbs vegetable oil
2 tbs flour
3½ oz/100g streaky bacon, cut into ¾ inch/2cm cubes
1 clove garlic, crushed
12 small onions, peeled
extra butter
fried croûtons, to serve
3 sprigs fresh parsley, chopped
FOR THE MARINADE
1 large onion, roughly chopped
1 carrot, sliced
2 tbs olive oil
bouquet garni of fresh thyme, parsley and bay leaf
1 bottle red
salt, pepper

Combine all the marinade ingredients and pour over the meat in an earthenware bowl. Leave to marinate overnight.

Remove the meat from the marinade and pat dry with absorbent kitchen paper (paper towels). Brown on all sides in a large flameproof casserole in the butter and oil. Sprinkle with the flour, turning the pieces over a high heat.

Add the bacon, garlic, the strained marinade and the bouquet garni. Season, lower the heat and simmer, covered, over a low heat for 3 hours, until tender.

Meanwhile, lightly sauté the onions in butter, then add to the stew about 15 minutes before the end of cooking. Serve in a deep dish with the croûtons and parsley sprinkled over the top.

BOEUF BRAISÉ

A perfect dinner-party dish, adapted from the world-famous braised beef recipe of Alexandre Dumaine, for many years the chef at the Hotel Côte d'Or, Saulieu. The best beef deserves a very good, but not your grandest, red burgundy: a Pommard, perhaps, or less expensively, a Santenay. Recipe of Alexandre Dumaine. Serves 6-8.

3½ lb/1.5kg braising beef in 1 piece
4 tbs sunflower oil
2 carrots, finely diced
2 onions, finely diced
2 leeks, finely diced and well rinsed
1 turnip, finely diced
veal bones, chopped
1 chicken neck
3 tbs butter
1 pig's trotter
2 tomatoes, chopped
salt, pepper
8fl oz/250ml (2 cups) white burgundy
bouquet garni of fresh thyme, parsley and bay leaf
12fl oz/350ml (1½ cups) red burgundy

Gently brown the beef all over in the oil, then transfer to a large flameproof casserole.

Sauté the diced vegetables in the oil remaining in the pan, then add to the casserole. Fry the veal bones and chicken neck in 3 tbs butter until brown, then add to the casserole.

Blanch the pig's trotter in boiling water for 5 minutes, then plunge into cold water. Add to the casserole with the tomatoes and season lightly. Pour over the white burgundy and cook gently until all the liquid has evaporated. Add the bouquet garni and enough red burgundy to three-quarters cover the meat. Cover the casserole and simmer for up to 3 hours, turning the meat occasionally, until tender. Serve.

FILET DE CHAROLAIS AUX MORILLES

Charolais fillet steak with fresh morel mushrooms. When fresh morels are unavailable – that is, all year except spring! – use preserved ones. With this drink an honest, rich Givry 'Clos de Vernlis' from the Côte Chalonnaise or a St-Romain from Alain Gras. These are both good wines of Côte de Beaune character without its fancy prices. Recipe of Jean-Paul Thibert. Serves 4.

4 7oz/200g fillets of Charolais beef
³/₄ pint/500ml (2 cups) red burgundy
3¹/₂oz/100g (7 tbs) butter
2oz/60g fresh morels
salt, pepper

Boil the wine to reduce by one-third, then thicken with half the butter, added in small knobs, beating constantly. Fry the steaks in the remaining butter, then keep warm. Fry the morels in the same pan.

Arrange the morels around each plate and place a steak in the centre. Spoon over the sauce. Serve at once.

ROYAL HUNTING

The good cheer is excessive, they bring dishes
of whole animals roasted; and for the pyramids of
fruit they have to heighten the doors.

MADAME DE SÉVIGNÉ

Visiting the seventeenth-century Château de Menou, its dilapidated royal suite in the process of restoration, I was struck by an awesome thought. If the Burgundian lord had to keep a room ready for Louis XIV just in case he dropped by – like others at Sully, Commarin and Époisses, was he also obliged to have his hunt permanently on alert in case the ubiquitous Sun King fancied a day's hunting?

The forests of the Nièvre were once the natural domain of partridge, roebuck, hare, wild duck and wild boar. Nowadays, with the flight from the land of game as well as countryfolk, the days are over when roebuck would be killed and become venison within three hours and probably be eaten the same day. And Burgundian hunting, for all but the privileged few, is an excuse for the long walk and tall story.

No one is better at these stories than our friend, Antoine Cornu. He tells of a hunting colleague who used to serve a seven-course hunt luncheon. After the entrée, fish, meat and game came a nice salad which, Antoine hoped, would be a refreshing pause before the cheese. To his horror, it came accompanied by a turkey. When Antoine protested, his friend said: 'But, my dear Antoine, a salad looks so sad by itself.'

A perfect pheasant in cabbage leaves, according to Antoine, needs two pheasants: one old and decaying, the other young and tender. The high one is cooked to impregnate the cabbage, then thrown away and replaced by the young one.

A victorian uncle of Antoine's was an insatiable gourmand. 'He would have a twelve-egg omelette before walking fifteen kilometres to the hunt,' Antoine told us. 'Then he'd walk another ten with the guns, working up an appetite for his twelve-egg *oeufs en meurette* (poached eggs in a red wine sauce) at lunchtime.

Then, another fifteen back home. What he had for supper, history does not relate, but he never had cholesterol trouble.'

I expressed my squeamishness about the shooting of larks to make pâté. 'But have you tasted them with truffles and foie gras?' he said, evoking the pleasure by a hushed gurgle of reverence. 'I have a three-page recipe so complicated no one has ever been able to repeat it!'

Hunters of the old school are scornful of new trends in gastronomy. 'You have to ask for a magnifying glass to even see your foie gras these days,' Antoine complained. 'And then it has a fig on top. Burgundian *haute cuisine* was once in thrall to the avocado pear which took over from wine, butter and cream. Now we've moved on to the kiwi. The Swiss, I hear, are converting vineyards into plantations of kiwi with which to smother our foie gras! *Kiwi en meurette* – I can see it coming – ugh!'

He was happier with his Dijon neighbour Madeleine Lecat's straightforward recipes for jugged hare, pheasant with chestnuts and even rabbit with prunes. And he would surely have approved of Dominique Burguet's wild boar *façon Dominique.*

Left:
Anteroom,
Château de
Menou, in the
Nièvre

Right:
Drawing room,
Château de
Menou

Well at St-Pierre Hospice (gastronomic museum), Arnay-le-Duc

Dominique's husband, Alain, is a keen hunter. He also cultivates $13\frac{1}{2}$ acres, yielding 30,000 bottles a year of Gevrey-Chambertin, not only the finest of Burgundy reds but a perfect match for game.

'It starts as a hefty wine,' Alain said. 'Only later does it achieve its smoothness and finesse.' A perfectly balanced Gevrey-Chambertin should not be drunk for at least ten years. It will keep forty.

In their village house's cosy kitchen, just off the *chai*, we tasted at 9.30 a.m. Whatever your doctor says, the great wines should be tasted without food. Big balloon glasses gave the young wine oxygen, so it could breathe sooner. And those complex aromas quite took my breath away.

What did Alain look for in a Gevrey-Chambertin? First, a ruby reflection in the glass – a certain depth and limpidity.

St-Pierre Hospice, Arnay-le-Duc

glory, Alain would be off to Grey for the roebuck, Châtillon-sur-Seine for the deer, doe and wild boar and even to Alsace when delivering wine to hunting clients. Hunting is a way of getting to know business colleagues better, he reckons.

And one of his clients was Jean-Pierre Silva, the Bouilland restaurateur. Himself a keen hunter, Jean-Pierre in turn went hunting with his highly cultivated goat's cheese supplier, Pierre Moine. 'Usually, we're so busy talking about some artist or composer,' Jean-Pierre said, 'we miss the game.'

Vineyard and forest are inevitably linked in Burgundy. *À la vigneronne* means made with grapes. Christiane

Ferme Auberge du Vieux Château, Oulon, in the Nièvre

The vineyards at Meursault, late autumn

Then the smell of it, far from obvious. You mustn't cheat: if there's nothing in it for you, don't guess raspberries.

'When you drink it with game,' Alain continued, 'there's a tendency to find stewed fruit – blackcurrants, blackberries and bilberries.' After the harvest, when turning autumn leaves give the Côte d'Or its renowned days of golden and russet

118

Gutigny did her quails with raisins and served them with a wonderful potato cake called *treuffé*. Antoine Cornu uses black and white grapes with his saddle of hare.

Although I have never found shot in a Bresse pigeon, I associate pigeons with rough shooting and it counts as a game bird. At Beaune, we had a specially good one at Jacques Lainé's.

By the way, we were fascinated to know the daily drinking habits of the Burguets, makers of such a prestigious wine; Dominique's parents were *vignerons* at Gigondas, so she was brought up with good wine. 'We only drink our Gevrey-Chambertin at weekends,' she said. And weekdays? 'Water,' Alain replied. He was not joking.

Ruins of L'Abbaye de Ste-Marguerite near Bouilland

CAILLES AUX RAISINS

Quails with raisins. Basically, this is a simple country dish, so serve any good Hautes-Côte de Nuits. High above Nuits-St-Georges, wines from places like Marey-les Fussey are upcoming and reasonably priced. Recipe of Christiane Gutigny. Serves 5.

5 quails
2oz/60g (½ stick) butter
4 tbs vegetable oil
salt, pepper
1 glass port
8oz/250g Corinth raisins
2 egg yolks
5 tbs double (heavy) cream

Brown the quails in the butter and oil very gently on all sides in a large flameproof casserole. Season, then flame with the port.

Pour in 2 wine glasses of hot water, add the raisins and simmer gently, covered, for 1 hour, no longer.

Just before serving, mix the egg yolks with the cream in a bowl. Heat through then stir into the casserole with the quails and raisins. Serve with *treuffé* (see below) or petits pois.

PIGEON DE BRESSE POËLÉ AU VIN ROUGE DE BOURGOGNE

Bresse pigeon fried in red burgundy. We ate this with a 1987 St-Romain from Alain Gras, a lesser-known red from the Côte de Beaune. It was rhapsodized by a local *vigneron*: '*O Saint-Romain, bold, robust, and so fruity, we like your freshness as much as your finesses.*' So did we. Recipe of Jacques Lainé. Serves 4.

4 pigeons, each weighing about
10oz/300g
1oz/30g (2 tbs) butter
2 tbs vegetable oil
1 carrot, diced
2 shallots, diced
1 onion, diced
1 bottle red burgundy
1 liqueur glass Cognac
bouquet garni of fresh thyme, parsley
and bay leaf
2 tbs caster (superfine) sugar
2½ oz/75g (5 tbs) butter
salt, pepper

Singe the pigeons to remove all feathers, then clean them, reserving the livers and hearts. Cut each pigeon in half and bone (or get the poulterer to do this). Set the boned pigeons aside.

Crush the pigeon carcasses and brown them in the butter and oil. When they are coloured, stir in the vegetables and lightly brown them. Add the wine and bring to the boil, then flame with the Cognac.

Add the bouquet garni, sugar and 7fl oz/200ml (scant 1 cup) water and simmer, covered, for 2 hours, until the liquid is reduced to just 8fl oz/250ml (1 cup). Beat in the butter in small knobs, then pass the sauce through a fine sieve. Check the seasoning and keep hot.

Season the boned pigeons and saute them for 8 minutes on the skin sides, then one minute on the flesh sides: this makes them soft and crispy at the same time. Add the livers and hearts for the last minute of cooking. Place the pigeons on four plates and spoon the sauce over each. Fresh spinach and sautéd baby spring onions (scallions) are the ideal accompaniments.

FAISAN EN COCOTTE

Pheasant cooked in a *cocotte*, a small, round casserole, with chestnuts and mushrooms. Eat with a sturdy red, like a Pommard from Andre Mussy, a *vigneron*

Toucy, birthplace of lexicographer Pierre Larousse (Gastronomic Dictionary)

of later years so handsome and dapper that, when he went to Spago, the 'in' Los Angeles restaurant, everyone thought he was a famous French film star and asked for autographs. Recipe of Madeleine Lecat. Serves 4.

2oz/60g streaky bacon, diced
1oz/30g (2 tbs) butter
1 pheasant
½ glass Madeira
15 small onions, peeled
6 chestnuts, peeled
salt, pepper
7oz/200g (3 cups) button
mushrooms

Sauté the bacon in the melted butter in a flameproof *cocotte* or casserole. Add the pheasant and brown all over. Stir in the Madeira, onions and chestnuts, then season and simmer, covered, gently for 1 hour, turning the pheasant over occasionally.

Fifteen minutes before ready to serve, add the mushrooms. Adjust the seasoning if necessary.

Carve the bird, then spoon over the sauce and serve. Brussels sprouts and chipolata (link pork) sausages are good accompaniments.

RABLE DE LIÈVRE À LA PIRON

Marinated saddle of hare roasted with grapes in a peppery sauce. This is Antoine Cornu's version of a recipe by Henri Racouchot, a pre-World War II chef in Dijon. Recipes cooked *à la piron* are in honour of Alexis Piron, an eighteenth-century poet from Dijon. Eat this with a good, firm young red burgundy, a 3-year-old Aloxe-Corton, or, less grandly, Pernand-Vergelesses. Recipe of Antoine Cornu. Serves 4.

1 saddle of hare
2 slices streaky bacon, diced
salt, pepper
3¹/₂/100g white grapes
3¹/₂/100g black grapes
1 tbs marc de Bourgogne *or Cognac*
2 tbs double (heavy) cream
1 tbs freshly milled pepper
FOR THE MARINADE
6 shallots, chopped
3 cloves garlic, peeled
2 sticks celery, chopped
1 sprig fresh thyme
1 bay leaf
2fl oz/60ml marc de Bourgogne

Spike the hare all over with the streaky bacon, them combine with all the marinade ingredients in an earthenware bowl and leave for 2-3 days, turning occasionally.

Remove the hare from the marinade, pat dry, season and roast in a 380°F/ 190°C/Gas Mark 5 oven about 45 minutes, until pink and juices run out if pierced with the tip of a knife.

Meanwhile, peel and seed (pit) the grapes. Put them around the roasted hare on a serving platter and flame with the marc. When ready to carve, stir the cream and pepper into the juices in the pan and serve as a gravy.

SANGLIER FAÇON DOMINIQUE

Wild boar cooked in Gevrey-Chambertin (when royalty is dropping by), or a more everyday, good red burgundy. This dish is excellent served with several purées, such as chestnut, carrot and potato. We enjoyed this with a Gevrey-Chambertin from Alain Burguet. Recipe of Dominique Burguet. Serves 4 or 5.

2 onions, roughly chopped
2oz/60g (½ stick) butter
1 tbs olive oil
3⅓ lb/1.5kg wild boar
1 liqueur glass of Cognac
1 tomato, roughly chopped
freshly squeezed juice of ½ lemon
salt, pepper
1 sprig fresh thyme
1 bay leaf
1 tbs flour
1 or 2 bottles red burgundy
7oz/200g (3 cups) mushrooms,
preferable cep or boletus
1 tbs redcurrant jelly

In a large flameproof casserole, glaze the onions in the butter and oil until they are golden, then remove from the pan. Brown the meat all over, then flame with Cognac.

Return the onions to the casserole, along with the tomato, lemon juice, seasoning, thyme, bay leaf and enough wine to cover all the ingredients. Add the mushrooms and simmer, covered, for 1½ hours.

Remove the meat and mushrooms, then simmer the stock, uncovered, for two hours to reduce. About 15 minutes before serving, return the meat and mushrooms to the casserole to heat through.

Put the meat in a deep serving dish. Stir the redcurrant jelly into the sauce, then spoon the sauce and mushrooms over the meat. Serve at once.

TREUFFÉ

A crispy potato cake made with cream cheese. A course in itself, but a delicious accompaniment, too. Recipe of Christiane Gutigny. Serves 6.

2¼ lb / 1kg potatoes, unpeeled
salt, pepper
4 eggs
2 tbs flour
1lb / 500g cream cheese
5fl oz / 150ml (⅓ cup) single (light)
cream
2 tbs vegetable oil

Boil the potatoes in salted water. Drain well and peel. Crush with a fork, leaving whole pieces.

Beat together the eggs, flour, cream cheese and cream, the add to the potatoes, beating in well. Season.

Heat the oil in a large frying pan (skillet) until very hot. Add the potato mixture and flatten out, then fry to golden brown on both sides. Serve very hot, cut into wedges.

ALL THAT CHEESE

A little garlic, a few white onions and cherries,

rock salt and pepper on cream cheese . . .

When you can't do better, what a way of

going to the country!

COLETTE

All that cheese can't be good for you, can it? Well, the Burgundians have survived their twenty to thirty varieties with a flourish. The staple diet of peasants and monks in medieval times, cheese now comes at either end of a Burgundian meal – beginning in a hot goat's cheese salad with a cool glass of St-Véran white or ending on a cheeseboard with your richest, grandest Côte de Nuits red.

There are even cheeses which have the names of wine villages: Montrachet and Ami du Chambertin. And a rare goat's cheese called Chablis. So never believe anyone who tells you that cheese kills the taste of wine – as long as the wine is powerful enough not to be bullied by the cheese. Aubert de Villaine, a director of the doyen of Côte de Nuits producers, Romanée-Conti, advises: 'I prefer to drink our older Grand Cru vintages alone to get their full nuances. But our younger Vosne-Romanée, Richebourg or Grands-Échézeaux go perfectly with a Citeaux. The monks knew instinctively what wine went with which cheese.'

At a Chevaliers du Tastevin dinner at Clos de Vougeot, the noblest of the five wines served, an '82 Latricières-Chambertin, did honour to the noblest of French cheeses, which naturally included Citeaux.

At the monastery of Citeaux, Prior Jean-François looked more like a scholar of illuminated manuscripts than a cheesemaker. In fact, he was both. As he showed us the monastery's fifteenth-century glazed brick library, he said: 'Since early Christian times, we've pursued a knowledge of things divine and human. Monks were practical, as well as spiritual; they had to be to survive. So the Abbot

The library building at L'Abbaye de Cîteaux, near Nuits St-Georges

House at cheesemaking town of Époisses

Etienne Harding would no doubt have welcomed St-Bernard here with cheese and wine of the abbey's own making.'

Although we were lucky enough to be treated by Antoine Cornu to a superb 1978 Corton with our Cîteaux, today's burgundy is too expensive for the monks. But the cheese-making tradition was revived by the Cistercians in 1898 and is now a commercial venture. Two or three times a week, the monks get busy turning their cow's milk into a strong forty-five per cent fat cheese which is pressed firm like a Robluchon. The rind is washed every day with salt water and refined for three weeks in the abbey cellars. It bears the European Community seal guaranteeing its monastic origins.

More down to earth is the production of Époisses. Officially made in the village of the same name, it has a number of varieties produced in other parts of the Burgundian uplands. Burgundian writer Henri Vincenot deplores the standardization of industrial cheese making: 'Every farmer's wife used to ripen her Époisses with her own touch. An Ami du Chambertin is another variation ripened with *marc de Bourgogne*. And Langres, a drier version with a strong taste.'

We visited the Berthaut factory at Époisses. As late as the 1950s Père Berthaut, a local farmer, revived cheesemaking which had been abandoned for five centuries, and set up production in his barns. Michel Doret, today's manager, said proudly: 'We talk of a Berthaut rather than an Époisses.' It is an entirely hand-

Époisses cheese, the rind washed with Marc de Bourgogne

129

made process. Five thousand litres of Monbéliard cow milk are needed for the 2,500 cheeses being processed at any one time. After maturation, curdling and drying at delicately controlled temperatures, the cheese rind becomes more and more orange as it is washed with increasing doses of marc and laid on racks of beechwood cut only when the moon is rising. After five weeks, a Berthaut gets the look of a full, orange hunter's moon itself.

Not all cheeses come from factories. In the Yonne's flat, rich farmland north of St-Florentin you'll see the sign *Fromage* hanging outside many a farmyard gate inviting any passer-by to purchase. Even a small, modern villa's garage had been turned into an artisanal *fromagerie* for a superbly made Soumaintrain. Jeanne Leclère followed another monastic tradition of frequently washing her cheeses with salt water. Soft inside with hard rinds, they were all sold locally – to restaurants or at the St-Flo' market. And she recommended we make a cheese tart with her Soumaintrain. Or eat it hot on toast with a glass of red Mâcon.

This last recommendation reminded us of the sheer size of Burgundy: the cheese and wine were made 170 miles

Left: Soumaintrain cheese for sale at farm in the Yonne

Right: Goat's cheesemaker Pierre Moine at Détain, Côte d'Or

apart! Anyone planning a gastronomic tour of the province should allow plenty of time. Whether dawdling down D roads in search of a secret cheesemaker or praying not to be breathalysed between Beaune and Nuits-St-Georges, where an over-optimistic autoroute sign warns 'No alcohol when driving!', it pays not to hurry. Or dispepsia and a speeding ticket (and worse) may be all you remember.

We were well into bottom gear by the time we visited Pierre Moine and his goats. At a manorial farm near Detain-Bruant, the gentleman-cheesemaker introduced us to his formidable billy-goat, Le Ministre, who curled his lip at us disdainfully. Among the goats was one sheep. 'He was brought up by them,' explained the soft-spoken, witty Monsieur Moine, 'and doesn't know he's a sheep. Rather frustrating not to be able to join in the cheesemaking.'

In the haunted seventeenth-century manor house, filled with heirlooms – tapestries, ceramics and a huge chimney with an elaborate mechanical roasting spit, *le seigneur* let us into the secret of his cheesemaking, begun only eight years ago. 'Each morning I taste every pan of fermenting goat's milk,' he explained, 'and from the most acid, I take a little lacto-serum to put into the other pans. The more acid the curd, the better the cheese tastes.'

Monsieur Moine's own favourite recipe: a bit of goat's cheese on bread, with an anchovy and sprinkled with garlic, then shoved under the grill. 'And give it to your girl, too,' he recommended, 'with a glass of big white wine like Puligny-Montrachet or Meursault.'

We found Monsieur Moine's goat's cheeses among the 200 at the Dijon shop of Simone Porcheret. Madame Porcheret is a legend. Her tiny cheese shop was packed with local cheese buffs. A Dijonaise from a family of market stall-holders, she pooh-poohs the idea of low-fat cheeses. 'Cheese is no longer made with fresh cream, so up to fifty per cent fat really is vital for a good cheese,' she claimed. 'Personally, to stay slim I eat little goat's cheeses on sticks.'

On the plateau of Burgundian cheeses she arranged for Carey to photograph, these were the *mâconnais* Bouton de Culottes (trouser buttons). There was also Charolais, pure goat cheese from Saône-et-Loire; Grand Vatel, a *Brillat-Savarin* made in the Côte d'Or; Aisy Cendré, an époisses in wood ash; Pierre-qui-Vire, another monk's cheese, also made with fresh herbs; not to mention L'Ami du Chambertin and Époisses, the old favourites.

My favourite was none of these. At a cosy country inn, Auberge de la Rolle, between Ternant and Detain, I had my first experience of Tiaquebitou. In a candlelit ambience of decorative clogs, dried flowers, jars of candy and open fire grill, I was presented with a small wooden platter containing cream cheese, a little jug of fresh cream, chives, shallots, garlic and parsley. I chopped and mixed according to taste. And later repeated the treat Chez Camille at Arnay-le-Duc.

Armand Poinsot once again gave us a useful tip: 'Arrange your cheeseboard like a clock. Then cheese can be tasted correctly, clockwise, starting with the lightest and ending with the strongest. It deserves the respect of fine wine.'

It is also worth noting: whereas many of the grander restaurants could be in New York or London for ambience, the Auberge de la Rolle could only be in Burgundy. And that's why we kept going back for its simple grills and garden fresh vegetables. And, of course, Tiaquebitou.

Right: Tiaquebitou – Burgundian cheese speciality at Auberge de Rolle, Détain

FROMAGE BLANC FRAIS À LA CRÈME À L'AIL ET AUX FINES HERBES

At Chez Camille or L'Auberge de la Rolle, much the same Tiaquebitou but the grander restaurant gives it the longer name. Recipe of Armand Poinsot. Serves 4.

4 cloves garlic, finely chopped
4 shallots, finely chopped
1 small bunch fresh chives, finely chopped
2 sprigs fresh parsley, finely chopped
1 fresh cream cheese, direct from the farm, if possible
¾ pint/500ml (2 cups) single (light) cream
salt, pepper

Combine all the herbs. Cut the cream cheese into 4 pieces, then pour over the cream. Season and sprinkle with the herb mixture to each person's taste. Serve.

TARTE AU FROMAGE

A cheese tart made with Soumaintrain. We ate this with a light, young red Macon, one of the few red burgundies made with the Gamay grape, better known in nearby Beaujolais. Recipe of Jeanne Leclère. Serves 4.

5oz/150g Soumaintrain, or a 45% fat cow's cheese such as cambembert, sliced
¾ pint/500ml (2 cups) milk
pinch freshly grated nutmeg
1 tsp cornflour (cornstarch)
salt, pepper
FOR THE PASTRY
8oz/250g (2 cups) flour
1 egg
1 egg yolk
4oz/125g (2 sticks) butter
salt

To make the pastry, put the flour in a bowl and make a well in the centre. Add the egg, the egg yolk, the butter in flakes and a good pinch of salt. Blend together with your fingertips. Add a little water to make a moist dough that comes away from the sides of the bowl. Flatten into a disc on a lightly floured board, then wrap in foil and refrigerate for at least 1 hour.

Roll out the pastry dough on a lightly floured surface and use to line a 12 inch/39cm tart tin (pan) with a removable bottom.

Add the cheese slices. Beat together the milk, nutmeg, cornflour and salt and pepper and pour over the cheese. Bake at 350-375°F/180-190°C/Gas Mark 5-6 for about 30 minutes, until the top is set. Serve hot.

SOUFFLÉ AU FROMAGE

A cheese soufflé recipe from a Dijon housewife. Though the cheese – Gruyère – is from the nearby Jura mountains and not Burgundian, it is used for *gougères* and that is good enough for me. This is special when made from fresh farm eggs from Bresse hens. Recipe of Madeleine Lecat. Serves 4.

2¹/₂oz/75g (5 tbs) butter
2oz/60g flour
8fl oz/250ml (1 cup) milk
salt, pepper
1 tsp grated nutmeg
4 egg yolks
3¹/₂oz/100g (scant ¹/₂ cup) Gruyère cheese, grated
4 egg whites, stiffly beaten

Melt the butter, then stir in the flour and stir for about 2 minutes over medium heat. Off the heat, stir in the milk, beating until smooth. Season with salt, pepper and nutmeg.

Simmer for 2 minutes, stirring. Take off the heat again and beat in the egg yolks and cheese. Fold in the egg whites.

Spoon the mixture into a buttered 20cm diameter soufflé dish and bake at 375°F/190°C/Gas Mark 5 for 20 minutes, until well risen but still wobbly in the centre. Serve at once.

SWEET TEETH

> *. . . a little shell of pastry, so plumply sensual*
> *beneath its severe and devout folds.*
>
> PROUST DESCRIBING A MADELEINE CAKE

Dessert trolley (cart): the very words conjure up the sad wastelands of airport dining-rooms, the nail in the coffin of a plastic meal.

In Burgundy, not so. Confronted by the miracles of Christian Lannuel's *chariot de patisseries* at the Relais du Mâconnais, La Croix Blanche, I changed my down-beat tune and wallowed in five slices of different chocolate cake. And this was not at all a grand, expensive restaurant; just a quiet former stagecoach stopover in the countryside of the romantic poet, Lamartine, who wrote of it:

Passers-by, here you can find at all hours
Innocent repose and happiness . . .
Here experience the farandole
Of a thousand-and-one delights.

For those with sweet teeth, nowhere could be sweeter than Burgundy. Goodies abound on the farandole, a veritable merry-go-round of different tastes. And restaurateurs tend to give you a *dégustation*, like wine-makers, a taste of a guess-what's-in-this-one and as many as you've left room for.

At Chez Camille, a group of well-coiffed ladies and manicured gentlemen with the smug air of local notables started their meal pofaced, grimly hidden in their menus. By the dessert they were partying convivially over their *gratin de fraises* – (slices of strawberry in *crème brûlée*); chocolate mousse with sharp black *griotte* cherries and shortcake; an unsweetened fruit salad of melon, pineapple and kiwi to clean the palate; accompanied by Armand Poinsot's invention of giant *tuiles*, crispy biscuits (cookies) of almond and cumin.

For wine, we were back where we'd started with a *Crémant de Bourgogne* whose bubbly lightness takes those irresistible rich *gâteaux* in its stride. Nothing wrong, by the way, in returning to white for the dessert. Just pause for a moment and rest your palate with something that

Right: Christiane Gutigny's apple tart

Left: Chocolate galette of Dijon restaurateur Jean-Paul Thibert

goes badly with wine like a salad. In a viticultural area as complex as Burgundy, pump the *sommelier* for the lowdown; never think you know, he'll maybe save you a fortune by suggesting some value-for-money regional wine you don't know. Like the *Crémant de Bourgogne* we had at Chez Camille, cheaper and much better than a mediocre champagne to finish off a meal in style.

Another dessert *dégustation*, rather more New Burgundian than Armand Poinsot's, was offered us by Jean-Paul Thibert at Dijon: strawberry salad with pineapple juice, zest of orange, lemon, fennel and celery conserve; chocolate *galette* with pears and caramel, and coffee ice cream; iced *bon-bons* of dark and white chocolate; wild strawberry jam with cardamom and vanilla ice cream; and just the best *crème brûlée* in Burgundy, if not the world.

Off the restaurant beat, Burgundian desserts may be less sophisticated but, in summer, Christiane Gutigny works magic with the fruit from her kitchen garden and the eggs from her chickens. The simple apple tart and *oeufs à la neige* are elevated above their humble origins; and it was

hard to choose between her redcurrant tart and that of Christiane Fayolle who added blackcurrants to hers on the menu of the Ferme Auberge du Vieux Château at Oulon.

Clafoutis is another fruit speciality of Burgundy. Larousse says it originated in the Limousin, and I thought it was Greek, but several Burgundian regions claim it. Paray-le-Monial makes it with unstoned cherries and calls it *cacou*. In the Nièvre, theirs is called *flamusse*, made with apples. At La Roche Vineuse, Saône-et-Loire, it contains a cabbage leaf, and Madeleine Lecat, at Dijon, just calls hers clafoutis – in the certainty that it originated at Dijon which nobody would dare to contradict.

For that, of course, is where *pain d'épices* irrefutably originated (by way of ancient Greece, China, Arabia, Flanders and Champagne). The house of Mulot et Petitjean has perfected the art. In the over-the-top decor of its fifteenth-century shop front (mock Romanesque arches, Renaissance ceiling, art-nouveau trimmings), the avuncular Monsieur Petitjean answered the tinkling entrance bell and showed us his sugary wonders – *pains d'épices* in the shape, of fish and donkeys, with almonds, blackcurrants, orange, moka. 'We had a big success during French week at Harrods,' he said. 'We're getting our feet wet abroad, but we're really too small a firm. France is big enough for us.'

Confiserie, friandises, bon-bons, patisserie delight Burgundians at mealtimes or in between. At the little tables of Marie-Thérèse Bazeron's Beaune emporium, full-grown men settle down to *chou rouge* (chocolate meringue, chocolate cream filling, sprinkled with cocoa) and *pavé anglais* (sponge cake soaked in rum with crystallized fruit and covered with green marzipan). Why *anglais*?, I asked. 'I created it for Queen Elizabeth the Second's coronation,' she said, adding sadly, 'When she came to Beaune, my street was up for repairs and too muddy for her to visit the shop.' Poor Madame Bazeron. Was no Chevalier du Tastevin there to hurl down his cloak upon the sludge? And couldn't they have found Her Majesty a pair of wellies?

No such problems plagued Au Négus, the famous Nevers *confiseur*. In 1901, the firm created its *bonbon*, in celebration of a visit to France by the Emperor of Abyssinia, known as Negus. Streets up or

Right: Mulot et Petitjean, Dijon – a paradise for the sweet-toothed

Pavé anglais (rum-soaked sponge-cake with marzipan) from Bazeron, Beaune

not, he never came to Nevers. Only this shop, however, is allowed to use the name for their caramel-and-chocolate delicacy; they also sell the bright pink *nougatines*, little almond mouth-poppers originating in Nevers as well.

To each, their own succulence: *corniottes* (apple and honey) at Chagny and Tournus; *cassissines* (blackcurrant and sugar) at Dijon; and the world-famous *anis* at Flavigny-sur-Ozerain.

Revealing aniseed in its secret recipe, this pea-sized pastille is made at a former Benedictine abbey. In their family home-cum-factory, the Troubats have been making *anis* in fourteen different flavours since 1923. But according to Catherine Troubat, daughter of the family, the pastille's origin dates from 52 BC. 'The Roman general Flavinius brought Caesar an aniseed medicament, which helped the Emperor beat the Gauls' Vercingetorix at Alésia,' said Catherine, pointing in the direction of the nearby battlefield as if it were yesterday's headline. The pastilles, in their pretty retro tin boxes, are even mentioned in *Love in the Time of Cholera* by Gabriel Garcia Márquez. 'They're my weakness,' Catherine continued loyally. 'And my weight proves it.'

GÂTEAU DE MOUSSE AU CASSIS

A blackcurrant mousse in a gâteau shape on a sponge base. Use blackcurrant purée or blackcurrant juice, not the alcoholic *crème de cassis*. Recipe of Christian Lannuel. Serves 8-10.

4fl oz/125ml (¹/₂ cup) milk
2¹/₂oz/75g (6¹/₄ tbs) sugar
2 tsp powdered gelatine
³/₄ pint/500ml (2 cups) double
(heavy) cream, whipped
³/₄ pint/500ml (2 cups)
blackcurrant juice
1lb/500g blackcurrant jelly, melted
FOR THE SPONGE CAKE BASE
2oz/60g (¹/₂ stick) butter
4oz/125g (heaped ¹/₂ cup) sugar
4 eggs
salt
4g vanilla sugar (put 2 vanilla pods
in a closed jar with the sugar)
4oz/125g (1 cup) sifted flour

Preheat the oven to 400°F/200°C/Gas Mark 6. Butter a 9in/22cm diameter cake tin (pan) with removable sides.

To make the sponge base, melt the butter, then set aside. Put the sugar, eggs, salt and vanilla sugar in a heatproof bowl in a *bain-marie* of warm water. Beat gently until the mixture rises and becomes shiny and pale. Remove from the heat and continue beating until cool. Fold in the flour and melted butter. Spoon into the prepared tin and bake 10-15 minutes, until a knife inserted in the centre comes out clean. Allow to cool.

Meanwhile, make the mousse. Bring the milk and sugar to a boil, dissolve the gelatine in cold water and stir it in, then add the cream and blackcurrant juice. Spoon 3 or 4 tbs blackcurrant juice over the sponge base. Spread the mousse mixture onto the sponge base, then cool and put in the refrigerator until ready to serve.

To serve, remove the tin (pan) sides. Spread with a thin layer of blackcurrant jelly.

PAIN D'ÉPICE

How a Dijon housewife make her city's spicy honey bread. Recipe of Madeleine Lecat. Serves 8.

4oz/125g (¹/₃ cup) honey
4oz/125g (heaped ¹/₂ cup) sugar
10fl oz/300ml (1¹/₂ cups) milk
1 egg
1 tsp ground cinnamon
8g vanilla sugar (put 2 vanilla pods in a closed jar with sugar)
8oz/250g (2 cups) flour
1 tsp bicarbonate of soda (baking soda)
pinch finely grated orange peel
butter for the loaf tin (bread pan)

Preheat the oven to 400°F/200°C/Gas Mark 6. Simmer the honey, sugar and milk for 5 minutes, stirring until the honey and sugar dissolve.

Combine the honey mixture with the egg, cinnamon and vanilla sugar. Combine the flour and bicarbonate of soda in a large bowl, then add the spicy mixture to it with the orange peel. Butter the loaf tin (bread pan) and spoon in the mixture. Bake for 1 hour, until the tip of a knife comes out clean when inserted in the centre.

Variations on a pain d'épice theme

OEUFS À LA NEIGE

Snowy egg whites topped with caramel, floating on a rich egg custard. Recipe of Christiane Gutigny. Serves 4.

2½ pints/1.5 litre (6½ cups) milk
8 eggs, separated
10oz/300g (scant 1½ cups) sugar
FOR THE CARAMEL
7oz/200g (1 cup) caster (superfine)
sugar
12 drops lemon juice

To make the caramel, put the sugar and 4 tbs water in a heavy-based pan and melt the sugar over low heat, stirring with a wooden spoon. Stir in the lemon juice. Bring to the boil and stop stirring. Shake the pan so the caramel colours evenly. When it is a deep gold, add 2 tbs hot water, standing back. Pour out the caramel onto a greased baking tray (cookie sheet). Leave to cool and harden, then break into pieces.

To make the custard, bring 1¾ pints/1 litre (4½ cups) milk to a boil. Mix the yolks with 7oz/200g (1 cup) sugar, then pour the hot milk over the egg yolks, beating constantly. Put over a low heat and continue beating until thickened; do not boil.

Whisk the egg whites until snowy. In another saucepan, heat the remaining milk and sugar and bring to the boil. With a spoon, drop dollops of egg whites into the milk and poach lightly on both sides. Remove with a slotted spoon.

Put the custard in a deep serving bowl and add the poached egg whites. Top with broken caramel and serve.

Tuiles géantes aux Amandes et au Cumin

These giant, curly, crisp biscuits (cookies) flavoured with almonds and cumin go well with fruit salads or ice creams. Recipe of Armand Poinsot. Makes 4.

4 egg whites
4oz/125g (heaped ½ cup) sugar
2oz/60g (½ cup) flour
2oz/60g (½ stick) butter, melted
1oz/30g (¼ cup) flaked (slivered)
almonds
cumin seeds

Preheat the oven to 350°F/180°C/Gas Mark 4.

Beat the egg whites until stiff, then fold in the sugar and then the flour. Fold in the melted butter and almonds.

On a non-stick baking tray (cookie sheet) spoon out one-quarter of the mixture, spreading it thinly. Sprinkle lightly with cumin seeds.

Bake for 4-5 minutes. As soon as the biscuit comes out of the oven, wrap it around a rolling pin to give it a curly shape, then transfer to a wire rack to cool. Repeat to make 3 more. Store in an airtight container.

Clafoutis

A classic recipe for a fruit tart made with a batter. Madame Lecat also makes this dish with strawberries and plums. Recipe of Madeleine Lecat. Serves 4.

8oz/250g (2 cups) flour
4oz/125g (heaped ½ cup) sugar, plus
extra for finishing
3 eggs
1¼ pints/750ml (3 cups) milk
pinch of salt
1½ lb/750g cherries, stoned (pitted)

Mix the flour and sugar together, then beat in the eggs, one at a time. Gradually stir in the milk, until the mixture is half liquid, then add the salt.

Pour in an ovenproof (baking) dish and add the cherries. Bake at 400°F/200°C/Gas Mark 6 for 30 minutes, until set. Sprinkle with sugar and serve.

Tarte aux Groseilles et aux Cassis

A tart made with redcurrants and blackcurrants from Madame Fayolle's garden. Recipe of Christiane Fayolle. Serves 8.

4 eggs, lightly beaten
7oz/200g (1 cup) sugar
3½oz/100g (¾ cup) flour
8fl oz/250ml (1 cup) double (heavy) cream
1 tsp marc de Bourgogne or fruit-flavoured liqueur
1lb/500g redcurrants
1lb/500g blackcurrants
For the Pastry
8oz/250g (2 cups) flour
pinch of salt
2 tsp dried (active dry) yeast
4oz/125g (1 stick) butter
2 eggs, lightly beaten
a little milk

To make the pastry, mix together the flour, salt and yeast. Add the butter in flecks, then add the eggs and mix with your fingertips. Moisten with a little milk if necessary to make a soft dough. Shape the dough into a disc, wrap in foil and chill for at least 1 hour.

To make the filling, beat together the eggs and sugar, then beat in the flour and cream. Add the marc or liqueur.

Roll out the pastry on a lightly floured surface and use to line a 12 inch/30cm tart tin (pan) with a removable base. Blind bake the pastry at 375°F/190°C/Gas Mark 5 until set but not brown (20 minutes).

Fill the pastry case with the redcurrants and blackcurrants. Pour on the mixture and return to the oven at 400°F/200°C/Gas Mark 6 for 25-30 minutes. Cool on a wire rack, then serve.

CRÈME BRÛLÉE À LA VANILLE

Burnt cream with vanilla, literally, but much nicer than it sounds. Recipe of Jean-Paul Thibert. Serves 8.

8fl oz/250ml (1 cup) milk
3 vanilla pods (beans), cut along the length
8 eggs, separated
2oz/60g (¼ cup) sugar
1¼ pints/750ml (3 cups) single (light) cream
2½oz/75g (5 tbs) dark brown sugar

Boil the milk with the vanilla, then set aside to cool and infuse.

Beat the egg yolks with the sugar until pale and creamy. Stir in the cream and cooled milk.

Spoon the mixture into 8 ramekins and bake at 300°F/150°C/Gas Mark 2 for 30-40 minutes, until set. Allow to cool. Sprinkle the tops with brown sugar and caramelize under a very hot grill (broiler) for a few minutes, until bubbling. Leave to cool, then refrigerate. Serve.

A Marc for Tomorrow

*A good meal should be as harmonious
as a symphony, as well constructed as a
Romanesque cathedral.*

FERNAND POINT, FAMOUS CHEF OF LOUHANS

We have come a very full circle. Here we are back at the Côte d'Or, Saulieu, cosy in front of a roaring log fire, thawing out the nip of a Burgundian winter over a coffee and a *marc de Bourgogne* to round off our meal. We glow with well-being.

Other *digestifs* would have been appropriate: a *guignolet de Dijon* (cherry brandy) or *prunelle de Cassis* (a liqueur of sloes). But a marc was really the most typical.

Marc de bourgogne is the distillation of skins and pips of both white and red grapes after the wine has been made – a great way of dealing with the leftovers. It is a winter process, and now, with the sky lowering black over the Morvan, our marc's fifty-two degrees of alcohol warmed numb brains into taking stock.

Beyond the rocking horse and ancient confessional in the hotel's hall, a portrait of Alexandre Dumaine, the great Burgundian chef, hung in the breakfast room, once the Côte d'Or's illustrious dining-room, where his world-famous braised beef was served to crowned heads and film stars. A 1948 menu showed classic Burgundian cooking with local products: young pike cooked in Montrachet; morel mushrooms in puff pastry; oven-baked Saulieu ham; a haunch of venison with chestnut purée. His counsel on the making of a good chef was classic, too: 'He first questions attentively the quality of his products, then how to prepare them. He does not neglect the honesty of his wines, nor the care which he owes them, so that the bliss of his guests will be perfect.'

How would Dumaine, we wondered, view the experiments of his avant-garde successor, Bernard Loiseau and the other New Burgundians? Kindly, I suspect. Although, traditionally, Burgundian vegetables tend to be part and parcel of a meat or fish dish rather than a dish of

153

Burgundian digestifs from Mulot et Petitjean, Dijon

their own, Bernard offers guests a whole vegetable menu! One we enjoyed started with cold mixed vegetables in oxtail aspic, followed by dwarf leeks with a vinaigrette, baby marrow flowers with aubergine (egg plant) 'caviare' in a bell pepper sauce and a stew of different mushrooms. 'But don't call it vegetarian!' he insisted.

A revaluation of the humble beetroot, carrot and pumpkin seems to be going on among the New Burgundians with lighter hands than their forbears. At Moneteau, Bob Waggoner has introduced a Californian touch to the kitchen garden of the Monte Cristo. His vegetables include yellow baby marrow, imported from the States and thriving; and his squash – the Cucurbita gourd – is doing fine, too. On his menu are such exotica as beetroot soup flavoured with watermelon, a

tempura of Dublin bay prawns with balsamic vinegar and Californian rabbit raised in the Morvan. The burghers of nearby Auxerre rush for these arcane delicacies.

The Auxerre younger set, however, may opt for the simpler pleasures of wine merchant Sylvie Chameroy-Boussereau's equally innovative bistrot, Le Quai. Firstly, for its position: right on the quayside of the River Yonne in that department's noble capital. Secondly for the formula: the matching of modest but excellent dishes with a glass of appropriate burgundy (and other wines): a plate of market-fresh vegetables with an Aligoté; carp and pike pâté with an Irancy rosé; black pudding with a Coulanges red burgundy; hot sausage and boiled potatoes with a red Givry. On Saturday night, reservations are essential. Sylvie is everywhere at once, chic and attractive, seating people and taking orders, never too hurried for a chat; she comes from St-Florentin and calls herself Florentine. Quite right: she has all the vitality of a Renaissance entrepreneur. And gives better value for money.

Exorbitant, however, were the prices in a chain brasserie in Beaune. Amongst the video games, juke boxes at every table and mock art-nouveau decor (Alexander Dumaine would turn in his grave), who is going to pay £40/$90 for a bottle of Nuits-St-Georges 'Patriarche' or more than £50/$110 for a Volnay 'Clos de Chêne'?

Such madness was explained by a young Norwegian, Christopher, who helps his Dijon friend and restaurateur, Jean-Paul Thibert, in the development of New Burgundian dishes and choosing the right wines to accompany them. Here was just one aspect of the burgundy price soar, but an important one: 'The fashionable new oaky style, so popular abroad, is very expensive. New oak barrels cost a fortune and it's another excuse for raising prices. In my view, it makes the wine too spicy, conflicting with the more delicate, lighter cooking of chefs like Jean-Paul. You lose the taste of *terroir*.'

But Christopher was optimistic. Despite the Burgundian wine 'factories' producing standardized wines that don't do justice to the great names they carry on the label, burgundy was resisting industrialization. Many older, smaller vineyard owners had sold their crops to the 'factories'. But a new, alert generation of wine-maker was fighting for their reputation. Bright young *vignerons*, jetting all over the world, have discovered that the best of their foreign clients still want burgundy with individuality and are prepared to reduce yields for better quality, paying attention to the intricate details of making. And, above all, personally supervising every stage of that mysterious metamorphosis of grape into fine wine.

A Lebanese oenologist, Guy Accad, for a long time was the wine guru of fifteen rich young wine-growers. His success was enormous. But even the New Burgundians in the wine trade are also traditionalists, distrustful of flash new trends. Wine-making is a quiet, serious business not just learned in a *Lycée Viticole*; you have to have a nose, a palate and a head for it, and no amount of scientific knowledge and hype can replace those. Without *le feeling*, the deluge.

Vegetable garden near Trivy, Saône-et-Loire

At Meursault, we met one of the most go-a-head of the young turks, Dominique Lafon. The family seat, overlooking the small vineyard of Comtes Lafon, had the low-key discretion of the best family producers. 'Always decant a great white,' Dominique advised us like a good clubman, 'a few seconds before serving.'

And if the Rabelaisian tradition of wine, women and song is still synonomous with Burgundian gastronomy, nowhere is it more so than in the wine trade itself. 'Some of my male clients expect to be entertained,' said a wine broker with a wry smile, 'at a brothel in Dijon. I get the bill – an itemised printout – but I can't discover from the coded items what on earth they've been up to.' The smile disappeared. 'Only the cost.'

Human appetite is the same, even if the menu changes. And in their personal tastes, the most avante-gard New Burgundian chefs proved to be traditionalists, too. 'At home, I eat *pot au feu, boeuf bourgignon* and a Bresse chicken,' Jacques Lameloise told us. 'In the restaurant, our dishes are assembled elaborately. So I love to keep it simple for a change.'

'I'm always on a diet,' laughed Jean-Pierre Silva. 'Tonight it's 0%-fat cream

Comtes Lafon vineyard, Meursault

cheese for dinner. I only eat my own dishes when I'm tasting to get them right. But sometimes I let go – an orgy of truffles and wild mushrooms, or Échézeaux and Vosne-Romanée, my favourite reds.' He was full of scorn for the English habit of warming red burgundy. 'Bring it from the cellar at 15°C. It soon reaches 18°C when poured out. And never drink a Montrachet iced. At 5°C the aroma is blocked, there's no flavour in it.'

Bernard Loiseau's favourite dish is fried potatoes. And you can't get more traditional than that.

What we had learned in Burgundy of its food and wine could fill volumes. Of its Big Six chefs, three were regretably not visited (Marc Meneau at St-Père-sous-Vézelay, Jean-Pierre Billoux at Dijon and Michel Lorain at Joigny); in a limited schedule, we had to keep space in our stomachs and pages for the lesser luminaries in *bistrots* and *ferme-auberges*, and for the Burgundian housewives whose recipes were graciously given and gratefully received.

We had relished the tastes of Burgundy old and new, and survived a surprise or two. Alexander Dumaine might flinch at the Pizzeria Snack Don Fernando (three

Street, Nuits St-Georges

EEC languages combined in one horrendous French fast food!) at Louhans; but surely he would have approved of Mère Jouvencaux not a block away, perenially turning out Bresse chicken in cream to the warm accompaniment of clatter and gossip and clinking wine glasses. *Plus ça change . . .*

157

INDEX

ACKNOWLEDGEMENTS

We want to thank all those who have helped us, either by lending their recipes or in other ways, to discover the many tastes of Burgundy.

Jean-Claude Astruc, Marie-Thérèse Bazeron, Paul Bélujon, Georges Blanc, Dominique and Alain Burguet, François Collin, Comité Departmental de Tourisme (Côte d'Or, Nièvre, Yonne), Antoine Cornu, Sylvie Chameroy-Boussereau, Clare Clements, Michel and Christophe Cussac, Vincent-Dauvissat, Julie Davis, Bernard Denis, Jacques and Christine Despierres, Michel Doret, the Fayolle family, Loïc Gallois, Patrick Gatinet, Alain Geoffroy, Georges Gugliemenetti, Christiane and Paul Gutigny, Russel Hone, Prior Jean-François, Gilles Joannet, Timmie Johnston, Dominique Lafon, Jacques Lainé, Jacques Lameloise, Pierre Langois, Christian Lannuel, Philippe Lavault, Beverly LeBlanc, Madeleine Lecat, Jean-Philippe Lecat, Jeanne Leclère, Bernard Loiseau, Alain Mahieu, Marc Millot, Pierre Moine, Thierry de Montalembert, Armand Monthelie-Duhairet, Sheila More, Colette Morel, Mulot & Petijean, Simone and Armand Picard, Armand and Monique Poinsot, Simone Porcheret, Jean-Pierre and Madeleine Quignard, Jean-Pierre and Isabelle Silva, Jean-Pierre and Lise de Smet, Steven Spurrier, Abner Stein, Jean-Luc Terrier, Jean-Paul Thibert, Catherine Troubat, the Vié family, Aubert and Pamela de Villaine, Bob and Christine Waggoner, Becky Wesserman, Colin and Pamela Webb.